Life *with* Abba Father

Life with Abba Father

Fathered by God for a Divine Purpose

J. Nicole Williamson

King's Lantern Publishing

Published by:
King's Lantern Publishing
Allen, TX

www.kingslantern.com

ISBN-10: 0-9851396-3-3

ISBN-13: 978-0-9851396-3-6

Printed in the United States of America

ENDORSEMENTS

J. Nicole Williamson has written another masterful book in *Life with Abba Father*. The absence of genuine fathers in the home, and the shortage of true spiritual fathers in the Body of Christ are pandemic in our culture. Nicole does an outstanding job of addressing these issues and providing great revelation of our Father in Heaven as a loving "Papa" who receives us as His own sons and daughters and draws us into an intimate, loving, and purposeful life-relationship with Him. Through the revelations of this book I have come to a greater understanding of my Father and to a more personal knowledge of how deeply He desires to relate to me as a son. I have no doubt that this book will warm your heart, challenge your present perception of God, and clarify your identity and destiny as you embrace the fullness of your Abba Father and allow Him to eternally transform your life.

Larry Burden
Pastor, Kingdom Life
Frisco, TX

J. Nicole Williamson has done it again! She has given us an insightful, Biblically-based, and very readable volume on one of the most important issues of our day, i.e., the issue of true fatherhood. Beginning with the fatherhood of God, she extrapolates the patterns, principles, and practices of authentic fatherhood in the family, the Church, and the culture. This volume, *Life with Abba Father*, will light a path for the reader to walk into his or her true identity, purpose, destiny, and inheritance that the Heavenly Father intends for all His children.

Jim Hodges
Founder and President
Federation of Ministers and Churches International

We all have need of affirmation, to have worth and significance. Unfortunately, so many live with deep wounds in their souls that have been poisoned by the devil's lies and deceptions. As we are on a quest to find our true identity, this book becomes an invaluable instrument by bringing us into the right understanding of God as "Abba Father."

In her book, Nicole lays solid Biblical foundations. As she shares her own testimony and gives us very practical personal applications, we can be equipped to live in the freedom Abba Father gives us as His sons and daughters, a freedom given so that we may live out the good plans He has for our lives.

Chris Juhl
Director,
CFN Fellowship of Ministers and Churches

To my parents, Mr. and Mrs. F.C. Bennett, who are now with the Father in heaven. I cherish every memory of my father and am grateful for the faith of my mother. My father taught me that *"All things work together for good to those who love God and who are called according to His purpose"* (Romans 8:28). And indeed, they do.

To Dr. R. Edward and Eleanor Miller whose spiritual parenting in my life taught me intimacy with God.

To Rev. John and Maria Miller whose love ministered to me the light that broke my chains of darkness.

To Dr. Randy and Carol Speed whose fathering hearts are an inspiration to the body of Christ. I will always be grateful for your leadership and ceaseless encouragement.

To all the other leaders whom God has placed in my life throughout the years whose influence has played an important role in developing who I am today as a daughter of God. I am grateful for your lives.

And to my wonderful husband, Ken, the father of our two beloved children, Daniel and Bethany. Thank you for your unceasing love and care for us, for being a safe place for our family and a godly example for our son and daughter. I love you always.

CONTENTS

FOREWORD

Our Heavenly Father has been raising sons and daughters for thousands of years. He is fully acquainted with our needs and struggles. He is able to bring us from spiritual infancy, through our spiritually formative years, and on to adult *"sonship."* He knows when our earthly days are finished and when it is time to be taken home to glory.

Our Heavenly Father makes no mistakes—He has a purpose for us being born into the particular nation, race, and culture, as well as for the parents He has given us, and has a sovereign plan for our wellbeing. We should thank God for them, and honor them.

We all need a caring, human father (or an equivalent) as early as possible in our lives to help us understand what God the Father is like as a Person. Remote, indifferent, unavailable earthly fathers can lead us to believe that God is also detached, unconcerned, and uninvolved in the daily cares of our world. God's Word, however, describes Him as a loving Father who is a protector, a helper, a father of the fatherless, and full of mercies.

In this book, *Life with Abba Father,* J. Nicole Williamson presents to us wonderful insights that lead us into the fathering heart of God. Nicole has put into words a true likeness of God as a caring, loving, and protective *"Papa"*—presenting to us, pastors, teachers, those who enjoy studying, and those who just enjoy a good book, a wonderful insight into God as our Father. I have known, worked, and ministered with Nicole for many years as a sister in Christ, and have watched the calling of God develop her as a gifted teacher, writer, and minister. Thank you, Nicole, for this understanding of our Father's heart in *Life with Abba Father*.

Dr. Randy Speed
Senior Pastor, *River of Glory*
Plano, Texas

INTRODUCTION

*"But now, O LORD, You are our Father, we are
the clay, and You our potter; and all of us are the
work of Your hand." — The Prophet Isaiah* [1]

I have often seen a difficulty with some in Christendom in relating to God as a near Father. Whether due to a lack of teaching or a negative experience with an earthly father, God is often perceived as distant and uninvolved. This is an important issue because how we perceive someone—including God—is how
we relate to them. God wants us to know Him, and be able to fully
relate to Him as an involved Father. It is foundational to knowing
our identity as His son or daughter.

I myself walked for many years as a born again, Christ-loving
believer before I experienced the intimate revelation of who God
is as my *Abba Father*. I knew the theology of His Fatherhood, but
without this revelation by the Spirit, the connection hadn't yet
moved from my head to my heart.

I have been a Christian nearly all my life, and have been in
ministry for thirty-five years now. I have served in church leadership in many capacities—through worship, missions, training, and
as an elder and Bible teacher, and more. I have lived on the mission field in Argentina, and have experienced true revival. And
yet, it wasn't until I was forty-two when God took me past my

theology of Him as a Father and into a deeper experience of intimately knowing Him as my *Abba Father*.

Until that time, I had experienced many encounters and revelations of God. I knew Him intimately as my loving Creator, Beloved Master, Faithful Potter, and Strong Deliverer. I knew Him as THE Father, but in many ways I did not deeply relate to Him as *my Father*, as *Abba Father*. Yet this was the very message that Jesus brought to mankind and is the heartbeat of true Christianity.

The way of salvation in Christ is a path that returns us to an authentic identity as Abba Father's children, and to a life of *family* bond with the Father, Son, and Holy Spirit. As His children, we also share a family bond and community with all who are in Christ. We are a family with a purpose and a Kingdom commission.

The intimate revelation of Abba Father and who we are as His sons and daughters is a critical dynamic to fully engaging our identity in Christ. It is the power of divine vision for purposeful living. The Father didn't send Jesus so we can have another religion, but as the fulfillment of His prophetic revelation to Israel as the One who would bring mankind back to original design. Father sent Him so that we might experience the life God intended for us, as His heirs, as from the beginning.

It was Jesus who has taught us the familial and respectful address of God as *Abba Father*. While religion reveres God as Supreme, it too often holds Him at a distance, too holy to touch, and too revered to personally call Him "Abba," meaning: "*my Father*." While some interpret "*Abba*" to be equivalent to the English words "*Papa*" or "*Daddy*," it is more than that. "Abba" is often used by Jewish sons and daughters throughout their whole lives (both young and old alike), in a family context, as a respectful yet informal term toward a father. However, it suggests more than a childlike relationship (as when using "daddy"), as it carries the understanding of close family bond along with a positional privilege as a matured son.[2]

In knowing Father God as *Abba*, we are brought into a deeper personal understanding of His Fatherhood over us: we revere His sovereignty Who gave us life and we look to His provision; we also understand the family bond we have with Him through covenant in Christ; we also understand the privileged status and responsibility we carry as His mature sons. [3]

Without question God *is* Holy, and we must guard our relationship with Him free from any taint of irreverence, but Father God also wants us to know that while Holy, He is both the loving Giver of life and the Father of a Holy Family—a family of those born of His Spirit who have an intentional purpose on Earth, and in eternity.

Since there is no precise equivalent word in English that conveys the full breadth of the important meaning of "*Abba,*" I will occasionally use the term "Papa" or "Dad" for the purpose of emphasizing the close family bond we have with Him. I mean no irreverence. I do this because the English term "my Father" may be misinterpreted as a formal relationship that lacks intimate heart fellowship. This would be contrary to the distinct privilege that God invites us into as His sons and daughters through Christ. He opens His arms for us to know Him fully as *our Father.*

In my personal life, I often call the Father "Dad" when talking with Him. It makes me feel close to Him, yet also reverential as I draw near to Him to know His heart and seek His counsel. God wants us to walk intimately with Him as we journey through life with divine purpose; He created us to be His royal children who bear His image and carry His government for healing the nations and ruling this earth.

According to Malachi 4:5, the healing of the nations is linked to a loving return of hearts between fathers and children. While Scripture depicts the end-times as days marked with wars, violence and apostasy, the prophet Malachi also declared that in the last days there would be a *return of the hearts* of fathers with their children. This current generation in America has been termed a "fatherless" one as many have experienced some form of separation from an earthly father; I believe we are poised for a needed return of hearts and healing in our land. The current chaos in cultures around the world is a desperate cry for such a healing.

xv

This healing, however, can only be fully realized by a turning of our own heart toward God as our Father to receive His intimate and purposeful parenting. Our homes and nation need Abba's fathering. Abba Father will teach us to how to receive His love and love Him in return, and through His love how to parent our homes and communities. He will teach us how to rightly relate to one another, how to esteem our fathers and mothers, and how to love our children.

The Heavenly Father has already shown us how His own heart is turned toward us when He sent His Son, Jesus Christ, to rescue us from our lost state in rebellion. It's time for us to know and love Him fully as His sons and daughters.

The Apostle Paul said that we have many teachers, but not many fathers. We need fathers; we need the revelation of Abba Father Who is the source of our true identity in Christ, for everything begins with the Father. The earth is longing for the manifestation of the matured sons of God—men and women who are *one* with Christ, and thus *one* with Abba Father; men and women who will *parent* the nations as Christ's body through the presence of the Holy Spirit, and with the healing power of Father's love, counsel and authority. For when this happens, the curse will be removed and the land healed.

I have written this book as a resource for you, that you might know the truth about God as a Father, as *your* Father. It is laced with the language of family that together we might more fully understand who we are as God's family, and thus our God-given purpose for our time on Earth, and in eternity.

May these pages serve to remove any block in your relationship with God and your identity as His valued child. May this book serve to help you move into a deeper place of intimacy with your Abba Father as His cherished child and heir who is here for a divine purpose.

Father, hallowed be Your name. Your Kingdom come, Your will be done, on earth as it is in heaven.

CHAPTER 1

THE SIGNIFICANCE
of a FATHER

"One father is more than a hundred schoolmasters."
—*George Herbert* [1]

Two things that most shape our life, choices, and direction are how we are fathered, and how we respond to fathers. This includes parents, spiritual leaders, authority figures, and most of all, God Himself who is the Father of all.

Our responses to fathers differ, and for different reasons: we love fathers, reject fathers, need fathers, run away from fathers, are hurt by fathers, are encouraged by fathers, are neglected by fathers, and are trained by fathers. But no matter how we have related to them, the bottom line is, if it weren't for our fathers, we wouldn't be here. Fathers are the most significant part of our past, present, and future. And the most significant father of all is Father God.

No matter how old we are, our lives are impacted by fathers—whether it be a dad, a coach, or a spiritual leader. Our relationship with fathers and responses to their leadership (*or* absence of it), influences our own leadership skills with ourselves, our children, within our work environment, ministry, or mentoring relationships. The more we understand our own need for fathering, and how to rightly relate to fathers—and especially to Father God— the more wholeness, fruitfulness, and divine purpose we will know and experience.

Fathers play a central part in our learning to govern in life. God gave fathers to be a loving authority for empowering a child's development as his heritage, and as those who also rightly govern. Father's matter; children matter. Sons *and* daughters were both created to lead and prosper the earth with divine purpose, and for this grand commissioning, we need fathering (Gen. 1:27-28; 2:21-24).

A dad's involvement helps both sons and daughters to be better parents, leaders, and influencers—those who shape the destiny of families and communities, and thus nations. It is a natural for a child to look to a father for guidance and counsel. In saying this, I want to make it clear that I am not discounting the mother's significant role too, but my focus in these pages is specifically on fathering, and most specifically on the Heavenly Father (I have other writings that reflect a woman's importance, as in *The Empowered Woman: Restoring Women to Their True Identity*).

Understanding God's role of fathering us, and how to relate to fathers He has placed in our life, creates a solid foundation for our life and success. Over the years, God has helped me to see His fathering care in my life, as well as heal any wrong foundations laid through the way earthly fathers have related to me, and I to them. We will look more at healing family dynamics in the next chapter, but first, let's look at the importance of God's original design regarding fathers and families. The more we understand God's *original design for earthly fathers*, the more we will understand *God's own Fatherhood* regarding us as His royal children.

FATHERS ARE AUTHORS AND GUARDIANS

The simple definition of a father is that he is an *"author"*: someone who causes something to exist, an initiator of life. All the dynamics needed to create life can be set in place, but it is the *father* who ignites the spark that sets life in motion. In Greek, the term *"father"* (*"pater"*[2]) refers to one who is the author or founder of a family, the progenitor of a people, including those he adopts or receives into his care and looks after in a paternal way. As such, a father is the provider and protector of a child's life and wellbeing.

The title of *father* can also refer to a man who *founds* a society that is **animated by the same spirit as himself** and for whom he cares in a paternal way with instruction and provision, and who actuates and governs their minds (ways of thinking).[3] A man who initiates and causes an idea, discovery, or invention to be produced and take on "a life of its own" is also known as a father.

All these definitions of a "father," describe him as being a **catalyst of life *and* caretaker of its destiny**. A father is both the *source of identity* for what he brings into existence, as well as being the *cultivator and guardian of that life*—preserving, protecting, and providing for what he initiates.

Guarding and advancing life was the charge given by God to mankind's first father, Adam, in the Garden of Eden (Gen. 2:15). Adam, made in God's likeness, was to rule the earth as His representative—governing together with the woman whom God had also fashioned in His likeness from the man and placed as the man's suitable helper (Gen. 1:28; 2:18). The man was fashioned to be an earthly father to bear the Heavenly Father's likeness. He was designed as a catalyst for life and increase, and as God's agent to prosper life in the way His Father would do—through love, for is God is love.

A FATHER'S IMPACT ON HIS CHILD

Fathers hold a foundational key to the wellbeing of a child. Their love, care, and blessing plays a key role to the maturing of a child's success in many areas such as:

Identity	Security	Purpose	Accountability
Ethics	Education	Guidance	Morality

19

Discipline   Character   Sexuality   Relationships
Vocation   Core Values

By these few dynamics we can see what an essential responsibility fathers have. God doesn't leave them to try and "figure things out" on their own for such an important work. God, as a Father, is a father's role model. He provides His counsel, presence, and strength for their assignment, as He does for each one of us — giving us His Word, love, and His Spirit to empower us for the work we are to do as His children. God's presence and involvement with His sons teaches them how to rightly father *their* children.

Because of a father's important role to prosper life, God says that children are to respect and honor parents through obedience (Eph. 6:1; 1 Tim. 2:1-2). I realize in writing this, there are some who have experienced a father's harmful actions or demands that are contrary to God's Word. While such demands *cannot* be supported, nor does God endorse such harm (more on this later), we *can* pray for that father or leader as God shows us what actions we should take to step out of harm's way.

Our response to a father's right leadership not only impacts our own wellbeing and destiny, but the wellbeing of those we care for, and the people we lead and influence. In our current broken world, our fathers and mothers may not be perfect, but honoring their good counsel is important for the maturing of our life and calling.

God has taught me that to honor Him means honoring my parents, too. Honoring them pleases Him. Even if a parent has been dishonorable, we can choose to act in an honoring way toward them.

From the beginning, mankind was designed to need a father's love and counsel, and someone to whom we are accountable. In the garden, Adam and Eve had a perfect Father—God—who gave them wise instruction. They had a perfect environment, and were perfectly loved. Even so, they disobeyed the Heavenly Father...a rebellion that cost them not only their intimate relationship with their Father, but the consequence of the man's sin led to the suffering of everything under his care, namely, the whole earth.

Satan works to separate fathers and children, knowing the impact that fathering has on the development of young lives, and thus everything that will come from those lives. He especially works to separate us from Abba Father. Abba sees a child's destiny and charges them to listen to a father (and mother's) good instructions, knowing it will affects a child's entire life for good and release the blessings of heaven over them.

FATHERING A CHILD'S DESTINY

A father's good instruction creates a solid foundation for their children's identity so that they can be released fully into their divine destiny. Psalm 127:3-5 says that children are to be like arrows shot from a father's bow—arrows that hit a specific target. They are to be sent with blessing to *be* a blessing.

Biblical values that honor fathers and a dependence on God's Fatherhood were once a foundation in American culture. They were seen as the building blocks for life and family. However, these family principles have been consistently replaced with humanistic philosophies that have eroded our cultural view of God as our Father and Creator, and thus our need for His guidance.

Darwinism, Humanism, and cultural individualism have promoted a *spirit of independence* that seeks "individuality" apart God's fathering. These have also turned our heart away from the need for fathers in the pursuit of "doing our own thing" and leaving home to *"find ourselves."* We've lost who we are as a father's heritage; as a nation we have lost who we are as Abba Father's heritage.

The impact of these ideologies are reflected in the rise of narcissism, corporate greed, and overreaching government control. There is no one to whom we are accountable, or to whom we look for wise guidance beyond our own natural reasoning. This "Fatherless culture" is reflected in the high rate of divorce, relationship betrayal, and diminishing moral values—core values of personal worth and dignity. It is seen through the rising number of fatherless homes, and even the twisting of what a marriage covenant is between a man and a woman. It is reflected in the increase of chaos and violence in society as a whole, and in the identity crisis being experienced in the hearts of many, and in the heart of our culture itself. We must return to a love for fathers through the love of Abba Father.

A culture's destiny begins in the home, and a home starts with a father. But without the father's love, care, and guidance the home is left vulnerable to destructive forces, like a house built on sand. Biblical values promote love and unity with a perspective of *inter*-dependent individuality within the family community—hearts that work together in connectivity. Social decay begins when we live as islands to ourselves, or in destructive ways of *co-dependence*.

Children *do* need to grow into the place of being independent with confidence in who they are, but a child's true identity is formed and matured through love, responsibility and parental guidance, not by doing one's own thing, casting off restraint...or worse, having to run away to escape some family pain. Children want to know their value, both as family members and as individuals. A child's leaving home shouldn't have to be a declaration of independence or as an escape, but of being prepared, blessed, and sent to succeed in life and purpose.

As a young person, I viewed rebellion and independence as the way to *find* my identity. I grew up in the 1960s and '70s, and was greatly influenced by a culture at war against any form of authority. Self had become our national idol. At the time, I also experienced a lot of family turmoil and inner conflict. However, through many hard lessons, I came to understand that a self-centered spirit was a wrong path—one that led to destruction and a *loss* of identity. Abba's faithfulness brought me out of the pit I had dug, and helped me to see that true identity is developed through love, especially within the family. They are not developed with the attitude, "Don't tell me what to do."

In loving care, God healed my heart and freed me from my self-destructive paths...and He did so by sending spiritual fathers and mothers into my life to help me.

FATHERS THEN AND NOW

In ancient times, the Mid-Eastern philosophy regarding family was often that of being a small kingdom within itself. The father was seen as the supreme ruler, priest, military leader, judge, and disciplinarian.[4] *As a supreme ruler*, a father's authority covered everyone in the household, including grandchildren and servants. His rule was as a *"goodman"* — the caretaker of all that pertained to his house with responsibility for its care, wellbeing, and prosperity. Every tribe, community, family, or even company of travelers had a "father" who was there to guide the group and prosper it.

As a priest, the father established the family as a corporate place of worship; and *as a military leader, judge, and disciplinarian*, the father established the family as a civil community. In this way children learned discipline, justice, and even warfare against raiding tribes. Children learned what behavior was esteemed as right and what was wrong within the community, and the reward or consequences for their behavior. A child's first training in warfare was by a father.

While a father was the head of the family, the entire family functioned together as a united community. This helped to give personal security, maintain family traditions, and involve sons and daughters in the responsibility for family work.

The pillar of family life was established by the presence of the father, but it was also impacted by the mother's influence and the delight and fellowship between father and child. One ancient custom that demonstrated the father-child relationship was the morning practice of children greeting their father; they would kiss his hand and stand before him to receive any instruction, or permission to go on their way. Then the father would customarily embrace each child, perhaps even receive him or her onto his lap for a warm embrace.[5]

Today's Western culture is very different. Kissing our father's hand probably wasn't the way we started our day growing up! Our dad may have hugged us or patted us on the head as we left for school, or he may have already left for work. Or maybe dad wasn't there at all, for whatever reason. Nevertheless, the *delight, honor, and fellowship* between parent and child—however demonstrated—is the cornerstone that builds strong families. It is what builds us strong as God's family.

Looking to a father for instruction, or being lovingly embraced by him may be foreign to some, but this is the experience that God wants us to have with Him. While God is worthy of highest honor, He also desires us to be close to Him, to know His heart, and be intimately fathered by Him.

The brokenness we experience with earthly fathers has often muddied the lens through which we perceive God as a Father. It is this clouded lens of how we see Him, and thus receive or reject Him, that He wants to wash with His love and heal with His truth. Abba Father wants us to fully engage with Him as His beloved sons and daughters, to stand confident with Him and in who we are in Him, for a life that glorifies Him.

The more we know and intimately trust our Heavenly Father, experiencing His good and involved presence, the more we will experience wholeness and success in the life as He intends. He is truly a significant Father, and we are His significant children.

Heavenly Father, thank You for the fathers You have placed in our lives, those who You used to give us life and who have helped us to grow and mature into who we are today. Thank You for being our Father, and for helping us to stand confident in Your love. We love You, Father.

PERSONAL APPLICATION:

1. What have your experiences been with an earthly father(s)?
2. In what ways have these relationships impacted your life?
3. Has God brought other fathering relationships into your

life to help develop you? If so, how have they impacted your natural or spiritual development?

4. In what ways do you relate to God as a Father in your life?

5. Do you tend to do things on your own, or do you seek the Father's guidance and counsel? In all things?

6. What is the destiny that you see before you for your life? How can it become reality?

CHAPTER 2

THE FAMILY FRAMEWORK

"My father gave me the greatest gift anyone could give another person, he believed in me." — Jim Valvano [1]

In the last chapter, we established the significance of a father and the impact they have on our lives. We got a glimpse too that fathers do not act alone in regard to families, but they are leaders whose love initiates and establishes a community — a unit of celebrated and connected relationships.

As we look more into the original blueprint of this intimate community that God designed, we will see it was fashioned to be the nurturing environment in which a child would be fully developed for life. We will also see that there is a blueprint of family life with Him that He has invited us into for our full development as His child.

THE FAMILY FRAMEWORK

The healthy interactions and love of a family are essential to the full development of a child. They work to create a *framework*, or "lens," through which a child views life. Our early environment colors how we process concepts and learn to relate to circumstances, people, God, and even ourselves. By definition, a *frame-*

work is an essential supporting structure that holds together a system or an arrangement of things. Mindsets and beliefs systems are an arrangement of thoughts that are held together as a framework by which we make sense of the world around us. **Our "framework" is a point of reference from which we operate.**

Our internal framework began forming while we were still in our mother's womb. Even scientific evidence shows that sounds, words, moods and chemical emotions of a mother affects an unborn child's perceptual and emotional development. Once born, our family structure of father-mother-child continues to shape our point of reference from which we learn to reason and relate to the myriad issues of life.

Childhood experiences, influences, and even personal response systems, both good and bad, all play a part in establishing mindsets that influence our choices and behaviors.

The family unit was the first and most important foundation established by God for our growth and wellbeing. It was designed to be the basis for empowering a life of relating to others through a framework of love and honor—teaching us individuality, yet inter-dependence. A community of love and honor makes a child grow-up feeling communicated with, connected, and confident.

Each family member is designed to contribute a specific dynamic to the family. [2]

- **A father provides** identity, safety, counsel, and provision
- **A mother provides** nurturing, comfort, and teaching
- **Children provide** help and a heritage for a father; siblings provide camaraderie and friendship, and older siblings help provide mentoring and care for younger children

A FATHER'S CARE

A father is the initiator of life and establishes for the child an identity through his *name* and who he is—his values, work, and character. His name, carried by the child, declares who the child is **connected** to. It contains a history for the child regarding where he or she came from.

In a recent movie titled, *The Good Lie* (a story based on the history of the "lost boys" of Sudan), two boys continually rehearsed the names of their father and forefathers. This was so they would remember their family identity in a time when family members were being killed or separated by war.

There is an innate drive in every human being to want to know where we came from, to know who initiated our life, who brought us into this world, and what they are like. What does our life mean to them? Do they love us?

As the initiator, provider, and protector of the family, a father's love and care creates an environment for a child to grow and feel *safe* and *supplied* with what *satisfies their deepest needs*. As a counselor and loving disciplinarian, a father establishes *vision, order, and direction* for a child to prosper with purpose. He also provides an needed place of accountability for a child's development.

A Mother's Nurturing

From the beginning, God fashioned the mother to work in unity with a husband for prospering the family. The father initiates life, but she brings that life into full development through her unique God-given capacities. Her character and tenderness is key to creating a nurturing environment for a home that is inviting, fruitful, and full of love. Her wisdom and teaching are critical for training the children in purpose and to engage responsibility from the heart.

A mother is a minister of *encouragement, comfort, and help*. She carries a key role in the training of a child's life. Some cultures portray a mother's position as only nurturing a child's physical or emotional needs or only caring for the home. But Proverbs 31 gives us a fuller picture. It shows a mother's work not only with the children, but also as a business entrepreneur who develops all of her abilities in prospering the care of the home.

When a mother cares for the home and employs the diversity of her gifts and talents for prospering the home, she models for the children the importance of developing their own gifts and abilities. Her faithful example helps prepare them for community life and service both inside and outside the home.

CHILDREN AND SIBLINGS

Children also have an important role. A firstborn especially is seen as the *right hand* to the parents. Their role is important in how they interact with the parents and *communicate* the parent's instructions to younger children. Older children are to help *care* for the younger children just as they have been cared for; they provide a way for younger children to learn healthy social skills of sharing and relating to others—helping them see that they aren't the only ones who exist in the world, and they aren't the only ones with needs.

Siblings provide companionship and *friendship* for life-learning and support.

A TORN BLUEPRINT

While the framework I've described of a father's perfect care, a mother's perfect nurturing, and a sibling's encouragement and friendship may be an original blueprint from God, in our torn world it may not be what we experienced growing up. The truth is that most families experience at least some level of disconnection or painful way of relating to one another. Some experience an extreme amount of it. These injurious ways can result in what is called *"inner wounds."* Inner wounds from family can act like filtered lenses placed on how we view life, our perception of God and what it means to be a part of His family through Christ, and even how we see ourselves (which we will look at in the next chapter).

Abba Father wants to mend our hearts and give us a *new framework—His family framework*. He wants to give us new eyes to see our life and world through His nearness and care, rather than through the filter of any unhealed pain of unmet needs created by family dynamics. He wants to bring us into the healing power of intimate relationship with Himself—the Father, Son, and Holy Spirit.

GOD'S FAMILY "FRAMEWORK"

The earthly family unit wasn't just some great idea established by God, it was a reflection of the loving community contained within God Himself. In Genesis 1:26-27, God said, "Let **Us** make man after **Our** own image and let them rule...male and female He created them" (emphasis mine). Holy Scripture reveals that "*Us*" is the Father, Son, and Holy Spirit. God is a One, yet He is Three in One.

God not only laced into mankind qualities of His own likeness, but He gave us the picture of His own likeness as the pattern for family relationship—one of being a loving and supportive unit. **Again, God is One, yet Three—the Father, Son, and Holy Spirit:**

- **The Father** gives us our identity, safety, and provision
- **The Holy Spirit** teaches us truth, guides our steps, and comforts us and helps us
- **The Son** is the Firstborn who shares the Father's rich inheritance with us, communicates to us the Father's will, is our Friend, and teaches us the Father's work

Each Person of the Godhead is *distinct* in personality and function, yet *They* are *One*—one heart, one mind, one will, one Spirit—They are one God. And when we are born of God by His Holy Spirit through faith in the Son, we are brought into God's *family* as a new creation, a new life in Christ.

ABOUT THE FATHER

Abba Father is the *Father of life* and beginning of divine activity. Our identity as created beings, and as God's sons and daughters, is rooted in the Father's love. In the chapters ahead, we will be studying many aspects of who Abba Father is and His relationship with us, so I will not expound more here except to say that He has provided everything we need for our full development as His royal and priestly children. He has given us life with a purpose and provision for it. His love and counsel give us confidence

31

and affirmation needed for success in life, and His guidance empowers our ability to prosper in all that He intends regarding us. We delight Abba Father's heart so much that we cause Him to sing in His joy over us (Zeph. 3:17). That's pretty happy.

ABOUT JESUS, THE SON

Jesus, is both Son of God and Son of Man, who *executes the Father's purposes* and *divine activity*. He is the **Firstborn** of many sons—those who follow Him and the leading of the Holy Spirit. He became like us in order to rescue us from our *lostness* and bring us back into the light of fellowship with God as God's children. He is called the Son and Firstborn because He came from the Father to us as the exact likeness of the Father. As Son of Man, He was conceived of the Holy Spirit, born of a virgin, and lived in human flesh. Because of His obedience to the Father, He was "brought forth" in resurrection power as God's Firstborn; crowned as the Last Adam, He is the beginning of a new family of restored humanity, that being the redeemed and anointed sons and daughters of God (Acts 13:33-34). We are a family of light.

On earth, Jesus lived as Son of Man, yet in intimate fellowship with Abba Father and the Holy Spirit. As God's "*Firstborn*" (and *Only Begotten*), He is the **Heir** who shares Father's riches to all who are brought into God's family through the *Spirit of Adoption*. In ancient Hebrew culture (the nation and culture to whom God gave foundational revelations of Himself), the firstborn son was the father's right hand and received the double portion inheritance for family provision. Jesus is the Father's Right Hand who brings us into our full inheritance from the Father.

The Son shows us the Father's heart and models for us a life that is "*Father-focused*," showing us what it means to live as true sons and daughters who worship the Father in spirit and truth. He teaches us to listen to the voice and leading of the Holy Spirit, who is our Teacher.

Our Brother is well acquainted with our weakness and is not ashamed of us, but gives us His same Spirit (nature) to love the Father, triumph in life, and do the will and work of our Heavenly

Father (Heb. 2:11). He calls us His friends, and shares with us the secrets of God. We will learn more about the Son in the chapters ahead, too.

ABOUT THE HOLY SPIRIT

The Holy Spirit is the third Person of the Godhead. He *releases the manifest power of God regarding divine purpose and activity.* While we may see some "feminine" attributes in the Holy Spirit's nature, such as being our Comforter, Teacher, and Helper, yet He is also associated in Scripture with POWER and FIRE! Scripture says that God is *neither* male nor female, and yet, within God is *both* paternal (fathering) and maternal (mothering) qualities. The Holy Spirit gives gifts *and* power to both men *and* women, and teaches both their governmental role as God's heirs (Acts 1:8; 2:4).

The Holy Spirit is the *Spirit of truth* who proceeds from the Father, and is sent to be our *"Paraklatos," our Aid, Comforter, Intercessor, Advocate, and One who comes along side us to empower us for life and divine purpose* (John 14: 16-17; 16:13-14). In Scripture, He has many names that describe His nature and His *expressed power* released into our lives for our full development and the work we are to do.

The Holy Spirit is known as: the *Spirit of grace* (Heb. 10:29), the *Spirit of glory* (1 Pet. 4:14), the *Spirit of life* (Rom. 8:2), the *Spirit of promise* (Acts 1:4-5), the *Spirit of adoption* (Rom. 8:15), the *Spirit of holiness* (Rom. 1:4), the *Spirit of faith* (2 Cor. 4:13), the *Spirit of judgment* and *burning fire* (Isa. 4:4), the *Spirit of wisdom, understanding, counsel* and *might,* and the *Spirit of knowledge* and the *fear of the Lord* (Isa. 11:2), and the *Spirit of wisdom and revelation* (Eph. 1:17).

I encourage you to take time to look up these Scriptures and ask the Holy Spirit to reveal Himself to you in each of these ways. Be prepared for a lifetime of learning who the Holy Spirit is in His important role of transforming you into the likeness of Christ.

The Holy Spirit convicts the world of sin, righteousness, and God's judgment (John 16:8). He shows us things to come (John

16:13), and takes what belongs to the Son and imparts it to us (John 16:14). He reminds us of His words. The Holy Spirit facilitates and enables the "second birth" experience for us to become a child of God and have access to enter the Kingdom of God (John 3:5-6).

While Jesus is the *Way* of God and the *Way* to the Father, the Holy Spirit is the One who *empowers* us to walk in the *Way*. The Holy Spirit is our divine Teacher and Guide who reveals truth for our sanctification in truth (John 16:13; 17:17). Sanctification is the divine work of grace that the Holy Spirit does in our heart and life—cutting away uncleanness and impurity in our soul, freeing us from internal chaos and dead structures (of demonic philosophies and false doctrines) that hinder us from walking in freedom and unity with the Father and Son.

The Father, Son, and Holy Spirit work intimately, beautifully, and dynamically together in us, for us, with us, and on our behalf, so that we might live as They intended from the beginning.

HEAVENLY PATTERN FOR EARTH

God's "framework" models for us an intimate unity in a paradigm of love and honor—one *that cuts to the heart of independence.* The relationship of the Father, Son, and Holy Spirit is our point of reference for living as part of His family. It is our point of reference for how we relate to the circumstances of our life—a reference that establishes us in a supportive network of love and divine purpose.

While the Holy Trinity is best understood through the metaphor of the family framework, the earthly picture is *not* a perfect metaphor: it is *not* to say that the Holy Spirit is female, *nor* is He the "wife" of the Heavenly Father, *nor* is the Son of God the "offspring" of the Father and the Holy Spirit. What this framework *does* provide for us is an understanding of the inherent unity of the Father, Son, and Holy Spirit in a community of One, and how we relate to God as part of His family in Christ—as sons and daughters who have a God-given purpose on earth. It also shows us the pattern for how He designed earthly families to relate together in unity, love, honor, and purpose (1 John 4:8).

FAMILY: PATTERN OF LOVE AND EMPOWERMENT

This loving community of the Father, Son, and Holy Spirit is demonstrated throughout Scripture. We read how Father *releases* the Holy Spirit and *exalts* the Son, how the Spirit *moves* with Father and *empowers* the Son, and how the Son *glorifies* Abba Father through *oneness* with Him, and how the Son is led of the Spirit to accomplish Father's work.

This heartbeat of love and empowerment serves as the divine pattern for us and our earthly families.

Just think for a moment how living from this framework would impact our relationships: Fathers would initiate life through love, women would be released and empowered for divine purpose without hindrances; parents would lift their children through love into success and divine purpose; men would love their wives and women would honor their husbands, and children would obey their parents. **It would be a community of love and empowerment with ever increasing fruitfulness for all.**

Perhaps this sounds too good to be true, a Utopia, nonetheless, it *is* God's original intent for our earthly families, and is certainly a reality in life with Abba. It is the living reality into which He calls us as His family. He has given us everything we need through Christ to claim such a life of love and unity. May we have faith to seize what is ours in Christ, and refuse the thief who comes to steal, kill, and destroy.

RESTORING THE FOUNDATION OF LOVE

It is sin that first altered our earthly family framework. It is the sin nature that continues to muddy our lenses and impair healthy relationship dynamics. Many people walk through life missing the foundations of love meant to be ministered through fathers, mothers, and family. Nevertheless, God has a plan for our healing and restoration, *and* for our families. It is a plan He put into place before the foundations of the world. He knew how the tempter would come, and how mankind would follow his own way. And so, He made provision for us, because He loves us.

It was the *Father* who initiated that plan because He sees our destiny. Our Heavenly Brother, the Firstborn, activated the plan by coming in the likeness of sinful flesh and condemning it on the cross. He did this so that we no longer have to live by what is broken and twisted, but in the empowering love of God for a fruitful destiny. The Holy Spirit comes to us to make this effectual in our lives. This is a beautiful family framework that operates for our full development and joy as Abba's sons and daughters.

I opened this chapter with a quote by a man called Jim Valvano who discovered a life empowering truth about the impact of a father's belief in him as his child. Every child seeks a father's affirmation. After all, if the one who ignited our life doesn't believe in us, why should we believe in ourselves? But the truth is that we do have a Father who believes in us—the Great Father who ignited all life and loves us dearly. And His affirmation trumps every other voice.

Abba Father believes in you and me, and who He created us to be in Him. It was for our full development that He enacted His plan to bring us not only back into relationship with Himself, but into His family community.

It is time for a new perspective—God's perspective regarding who we are as His children on earth. It's time to enter a new place of being fathered by Abba, and embrace the power of *family* wholeness into which Christ brings us. We are born of God to be cherished sons and daughters—a royal community who carry out our Father's governing desires on earth as it is in heaven.

Father, thank You for healing our broken patterns and for giving us a new framework in relationship with You. Thank You for restoring the foundation of our life through Your love.

PERSONAL APPLICATION:

1. How would you describe your earthly family relationships when growing up?

2. How would you describe your relationship with Abba Father?

3. How would you describe your relationship with Jesus?

4. How would you describe your relationship with the Holy Spirit?

5. How would you describe your connection to the body of Christ?

CHAPTER 3

WHEN EARTHLY FAMILIES FAIL

"Family is the most important thing in the world."
— Princess Diana [1]

God designed the family to be a safe place where a child can live and grow. A baby comes into this world anticipating to be received by loving hands that will celebrate and care for him or her. The potential within them searches for who will help them grow. How do I know this? Just ask any adult still dealing with the painful effects of hands that were not always loving, or perhaps not there to celebrate them. God's hands, however, are loving hands that are ever present and celebrates us as His child.

Human failures are a part of this broken world. We all fail in one way or another. Even so, we look for those who will love us in all our shortcomings, and who will walk through life with us. We look for connection, and hopefully safe connection. Safe connection doesn't always mean relationships free of conflict, but it does mean we are committed to love and to work out our issues, especially within the family.

Willingness to acknowledge wrongs, make things right, support one another, and extend forgiveness are what our hearts look for in close relationships. Neglect of these leave the heart bleeding and bruised.

Failings are a part of human nature and we experience them in every relationship—inside and outside of family. Fathers, mothers, extended family members, teachers, spiritual leaders, and others who we look to for our care can leave a lasting imprint, either good or bad. Rejection, negative words, and hurtful actions can leave bruises on our hearts and minds, especially if there has been no amends made. These wounds can make us feel distrustful and drive us to seek personal solace in unhealthy ways.

Wounds of the heart can compel us to disconnect from others and build walls around our feelings (and life). These walls, however, though trying to keep out the "bad," serve to wall in the pain, as well as hinder our receiving good from God or others.

The truth is that no matter who has wounded us, a child's bottom-line is often: *where is dad?* He is, after all, the one who gave us life and we look to him to be our protector.

WHERE ARE YOU?

Most of us have posed that same question, if not regarding our earthly father, perhaps with God: *"Where are You?"* Fathers are supposed to protect us and make us feel secure. Because the family structure is a model meant to teach us a healthy perspective of God's own involvement with us, hurtful family dynamics can impair how we relate to God as our Father. It can also impair the way we relate to ourselves, and who we are, especially if we *internalize* negative words and actions, or a parent's absence.

Wounds of the heart experienced within the family can build wrong perceptions that may be reflected as: "God is distant, I'm worthless, and I have no purpose." These emotional wounds become the fertile soil where Satan plants his lies in our minds about God and ourselves. We may even blame God for what we perceive to be as His lack of protection or seeming indifference, or perhaps absence. Though we may recognize our need to forgive others who hurt us, mistrust of God may still lie hidden beneath the surface of our thoughts.

THE "FATHERLESS" FRAMEWORK

In the book of Genesis, when mankind sinned they fell into a state of separation from God. Their spirit died and their *intimate* connection with Him was broken. This was the result of agreeing with the deceptive words of the serpent, Satan, who works like a python spirit to crush out life. This disconnection from the Creator Father established a new point of reference for wayward humanity—one's *self*, which happens to be Satan's point of reference.

This separation from the Father altered man's perspectives in establishing a new framework...a "Fatherless" or "orphan" framework. Instead of seeing God as his Parent and source for living, mankind now looked to himself as the source for meeting his own needs. Since the Father's love is the anchor of human identity, man's fallen condition set in motion a desperate quest to find that place of wellbeing through his own means. His new framework was now structured in an "orphan" mindset.

In the "orphan" framework, a person looks to his *own* understanding to meet his needs. This lens causes responses to spring from a self-protective and self-serving means to meet valid needs and desires, rather than trusting the Father's love and guidance.

Living by an fatherless framework can make us feel that:

- I need to create my own identity
- I need to create my own sense of security
- I need to make my own provision
- I need to provide my own comfort
- I survive by being independent
- I have no one to guide me but me
- I decide what is "truth"
- I make my own connections

When we try to meet our deepest needs by our own faulty human reasoning, we become vulnerable to spirits of fear, greed, self-gratification, and selfish ambition. **And where divine love**

ceases to be the central power in the heart, the door of our mind stands open to thoughts from the wicked one.

Since the Fall in the Garden of Eden, the earth has languished under the dominion of sin and death. Every human being is born into a broken world and with a self-centered nature—a *sin-nature*. The word *"sin"* (Grk. *"hamartia"*) means: to *be outside* of fellowship, to *wander* from honor, to *violate* God's law, and to err and *miss the target*. What is the *"target"*? Romans 3:23 tells us that our "target" is to know God's glory—the radiance of His love, compassion, and kindness toward us. The target is to be bonded with Him in love, as His children, and governing the earth with His dominion.

Operating from a *"Fatherless"* (orphan) perspective misses the life God intends for us. Sin falls short of the perfect bond of love between Abba Father and us. The power of sin is the self-nature, which is a bond (covenant) breaker. But we were created to experience life through the covenant bond of unhindered love—to love and be loved. Sin is what causes relationships to fail. Sinful responses to another's sin also perpetuates the harmful patterns within the family. I know this by painful experience.

The truth is that within the setting of a now fallen world, our *expectations* of being *perfectly loved* by another human can never be *fully* met. Only the love of God, can satisfy our greatest need and fill our deepest void. And His love never fails. Even so, God's perfect love doesn't always prevent painful things from happening in this world. What Abba Father's love does provide is healing, restoration, and hope, and even miracles. I also know this by experience.

FALSE JUDGMENTS AND VOWS

Wounds in the heart are the devil's playground. When broken expectations or ill-treatment is perceived through the lens of *self*, our soul can quickly fill with resentment. Satan likes to sow lies in our minds about God, us, what others think of us, and what another's motives *may* be toward us. He loves to foster chaos and discord.

When something hurtful happens, or is *perceived* as hurtful, how do we view the situation? How do we view others involved? How do we view God in the matter? Do we see Him distant and uncaring, or present and ready to help? How do we see ourselves in the situation? Are we the helpless victim? Or is there victory in store for us? **Painful circumstances bring to the surface what is in us, and exposes what framework is directing our thoughts.**

A "fatherless" framework pushes us toward a false means of self-protection. We blame, make judgments, and angrily spew ungodly vows because of what another has done to us. These keep us in the cycle of pain. For our judgments against others to be true, we would have to know *all* things—including another's heart and motives, as well as the past experiences that have shaped their own lenses and formed their "buttons" that get pushed. But we don't know everything. We struggle enough to know the depths of our *own* soul, let alone another's.

But God knows, so He says to leave judgment to Him. That may be easier said than done, but for healing to happen within us, we must let go of judgments easily made against those who have hurt us—whether real or perceived.

For healing to take place in our lives, ungodly vows must also be renounced that may have accompanied those judgments. Ungodly judgments and vows are accusations rooted in condemnation of another. God is not an accuser...that is what Satan does—that python that squeezes the life out of everything, and who stands before God accusing us night and day. *Unrighteous* judgments and vows are a partnership with him.

Judgments and vows may be expressed as: *"My father is mean and unfair—I'll never be like him,"* or *"That leader hurt me—I'll never trust authority again,"* or *"People always hurt others—I'll never be close to anyone again."* We even make unrighteous vows about God such as, *"You didn't stop that from happening—I'll never trust You again."*

These kind of declarations, whether verbally or internally spoken, keep *us* locked in a self-inflicted prison of lies and half-truths. How so? For example, "never being like a mean father" negates any of the good that father may have been; it nullifies objectivity regarding the root of his behavior and denies the healing power of love that is able to restore him and the relationship.

Such judgments establish an internal root of unforgiveness, and sets the soul on a secret course of working to fulfill the vow.

HIDDEN STRONGHOLDS

Satan exploits our emotional wounds to form strongholds in our thinking by whispering his lies in *vulnerable* moments. A stronghold is an internal network of thoughts that, though initiated by external circumstances, are solidified as "truth" through *our agreement with that thought*. Strongholds are thinking patterns based on a lie or half-truth that govern our perceptions and choices. They are fortified by rehearsing the thought over and over.

Scripture says that Satan is the father of lies and is a murderer from the beginning (John 8:44). His lies create a framework that is absent of God's truth and love. It is a lens from which the *natural* mind draws imperfect conclusions and makes faulty choices.

Faulty strongholds are a destructive framework that hurts individuals and families, and thus *destinies*. That is why God desires truth to be in our inward man (Ps. 51:6).

As children, we tend to forgive easily, hope expectantly, and trust blindly. But when offenses are repeated and wounds go unhealed, feelings of disconnection can invade the soul creating a darkened sense of personal worth. Insecurity and rejection infiltrate our view of our identity. We may even interpret unhealthy family dynamics as the way God thinks about us. And so we look to meet our own needs.

By the time we are adults we may have repressed or even forgotten hurtful things that happened. We move on—but not really. Lies that entered through an emotional wound may be operating as a hidden stronghold. The power of ungodly judgments and vows, too, remain operative until they are recognized, renounced, and put under the blood of Jesus.

Strongholds often show up as difficulties in relationships, a negative view of ourselves, or negative cycles in circumstances, or how we relate with God. We may struggle with a pattern of failures in one area or another, feel like we continually hit a wall, or self-sabotage our own success or progress.

MY DARK PRISON

Unhealed wounds of the heart are like having an infection—you may not know what the problem is, but you feel the fever and pain that ravages your soul. As a teenager I was angry at the world. I was rebellious, and at one point even suicidal. I was miserable, but I couldn't have told you why at the time.

A pastor (in trying to help me) asked if I thought my parents were a factor in my struggles. I shook my head no; I viewed my parents as good Christians, and they were. I knew they loved me, in spite of the fact that I had conflicts with my mother and my parents themselves had conflicts, in fact, our whole family had conflicts that often weren't resolved. But I saw that as normal family behavior. Life, after all, is full of conflicts. I felt that I alone was the cause of my problems, but I didn't know how to fix myself, because I didn't know why I hurt inside.

I look back now and see how I had internalized rejection, fear, and a negative view of myself—perceptions from some unhealthy family dynamics, though I didn't understand that at the time. It was a hidden infection in my soul—a pain I tried to deal with through unhealthy means. However, the more I did, the more the darkness grew until self-hatred swallowed my soul.

I didn't realize how self-pity and rebellion were reinforcing the stronghold of dark thinking. Being a Christian, I knew my actions were wrong, so guilt and condemnation deepened my decent in darkness. I was mad at the world because I felt worthless.

Isn't it strange how we can hurt inside and get mad at everyone one else? How true the saying is: "Hurting people hurt people," because they don't know what to do with their pain. They may not even be able to say why they hurt. I couldn't. I couldn't see clearly in the midst of my internal storm.

It takes the light of the Holy Spirit to uncover the lies that we have believed as truth, but are not. It takes the light of the Holy Spirit to reveal what is really true. Satan can twist even the most perfect circumstance, and so can our natural reasoning. Again, look at the Garden of Eden.

Satan exploits any event he can to sway our thinking away from light and love. He exploits our emotions to create destruction. That is, after all, one of his names: Abbadon — father of destruction. While Satan works to ensnare our mind, the root of our pain is our agreement with him, and with the lie.

While we cannot change our past, we can change our present, and our future. We do this by asking the Holy Spirit to give us light and teach us how to identify strongholds, and then demolish their power over us with the authority Christ gives us. In 2 Corinthians 10:4-5 Paul says, "For the weapons of our warfare are not of the flesh, but divinely powerful for the destruction of fortresses [strongholds}. We are destroying speculations and every lofty thing raised up against the knowledge of God, and we are taking every thought captive to the obedience of Christ" (clarification mine).

In Christ, we ARE *more* than overcomers. We have authority over darkness, but we must see the darkness and *exercise* our authority over it. To see it clearly, we must have a right framework. My problem was that I agreed with the darkness; I was living from the "fatherless" framework of self in trying to meet my own needs.

FREEDOM IN THE LIGHT

My parents were imperfect, just as I was an imperfect child with an imperfect response system, but they were also praying parents. I had just turned twenty when I was invited to go to Argentina and be under the ministries of Dr. R. Edward and Eleanor Miller and their son, John, and his wife, Maria.

The well of revival was open and the power of God's presence drew me into a time of deep transformation. I lived and worked as a missions secretary on the campus of a small Bible School in Mar del Plata, next to their missions' orphanage. For three years I had no radio, television, or the pull of worldly friends. What I did have was the empowering influence of godly mentors, God's Word, and God's presence in powerful services coupled with incredible encounters with Him through intense praise and deep worship. I also had Abba Father's love that didn't leave one dark rock unturned.

My heavenly Father loved me and wanted me free. And so Father began stripping away the many false patterns of thinking I had trusted in and clung to. At first I felt utterly empty and hopelessly lost in the depth of my darkness. I couldn't feel the presence of God that I saw others experiencing in services. I wanted to touch Him, but there was a veil that kept me from entering the glory I saw on other's faces in the revival services.

One night, during the student's chapel service, the pastor had the other young people surround me to intercede for my needed breakthrough. As they prayed, the lights suddenly went out, but only in that room. The darkness was *unnatural* and thick. Everyone felt it. I recognized the sinister presence as the same that had often haunted me in my room at night, back home.

The prayers grew in intensity. After awhile, the pastor stepped close to me and said, "Nicole, *you* have to pray. *You* have to fight." I was so locked up inside that it took some time before I could even open my mouth and pray anything. I knew, however, that I was fighting for my life against a very real and dark presence that was warring against me.

My prayer seemed weak—more pitiful than powerful, but it was a first step toward the light as I said, "*I break agreement with darkness! I yield myself to You, Lord!*" After that night, I found a fresh freedom in prayer and ability to read the Word, which I hadn't had in a long time…in years. It was a beginning to the shattering of my strongholds.

How important is our support and encouragement of one another in life's battles. My steps toward freedom were empowered by a family of believers in Christ, and of my destiny in Him.

I began to spend as much time in prayer and Scripture as I could. Every time there was a service I was there. I didn't want just a "touch" from God—I wanted transformation. I wanted to walk with God. I wanted to know His glory. I wanted to be free from my prison—completely free, and completely whole.

My journey of freedom was not an instantaneous liberation as the chains clung tightly to my hands and feet. Breakthrough came as a process of line upon line. Nevertheless, God gave me a promise that if I sought Him, I would find Him when I sought Him with *all my heart* (Jer. 29:13). He wanted my heart . . . all of it. So I set my eyes on Him and pressed in to Him with all I knew how.

As the months passed, I cultivated a deep personal dependence on the work and presence of the Holy Spirit. As I did, revelation came, and so did a deep brokenness in humility before God. Tears of repentance flowed from deep inside me as the Spirit of truth became my candle, exposing my self-will and rebellion for what it was—agreement with darkness.

I learned that the ways of darkness and self are many. He showed me where self was enthroned, and where my thoughts and actions operated apart from His love. I was convicted of my many areas of disobedience, though not with condemnation, but with a conviction and call to "come up higher." He drew me closer to Himself in a nearness that evokes change in the human heart. His conviction was an invitation to transformation through fellowship.

Like a brilliant light, God's love shown into the inward parts of my spirit, mind, and soul. I found that God's truth is like a two-edged sword. He showed me the beauty of who He is, and at the same time I saw myself and my sin—what was contrary to His own nature. And yet, I felt absolutely loved as He also showed me who I am as Christ's cherished bride, one that needed to be washed and made ready to walk through eternity at His side.

I saw the hardness in my heart. I saw the pride and self-centeredness and how they had separated me from the One who had made me for His delight and purposeful plans. I saw the darkness I had agreed with, and I began to hate it. I desired a right spirit—I wasn't made for darkness; I was created for the Light.

In His light I saw light and how much He loved me. His light opened my to see the lies I had agreed with. My prison of darkness was breaking apart by the power of Love's light.

God's holiness is terribly pure, and at the same time inexplicably beautiful. It makes you no longer concerned about another's sin—you simply see the evil of your own *ways* and you want to be rid of everything that defiles you. You want to run to Him, not away from Him, knowing that only He can free you of what binds you, and stains you. Only He can make you whole.

The Spirit of truth led me out of my ignorance and tore the veil of deception that had shrouded my thinking. I had been blinded by lies, but God showed me truth, and His glory. I knew I couldn't have *my* ways *and* His glory, too. I had to choose.

Jesus lovingly took me by the hand and led me to His cross. There He washed me in the fountain of His precious blood, washing away the years of pain and bitterness. Then one day—a moment I'll never forget—my chains fell off. I heard them fall... and I was free.

That unforgettable moment came during a worship service. The Lord had spoken to me prior that He wanted me to open my heart and praise Him, out loud—a common practice in quiet times of worship during services there. I was used to praising, but not in a way that would stand out. But He was relentless and wanted my obedience. I was afraid, but I finally gave Him my "yes." As we were singing, the music lowered and as it did, Jesus suddenly appeared to me. It was as if He and I were the only ones in the room. I opened my heart and began to pour out my gratitude (in perfect Spanish) for all He had ever done for me. As I did, I literally felt chains break off of me and fall. It's the only way I can describe it. And I've never been the same since that moment.

WHAT WE BELIEVE SHAPES OUR LIFE

True life transformation and healing comes when we turn from the love of self in response to the love of God. As a child, I interpreted others' actions toward me as saying, "You are worthless." I embraced a felt opinion that was not rooted in love. And I, in turn, responded unlovingly...actually, horribly at times! We can never prevent the unloving opinions or actions of another, but our heart *can* be rooted in the healing Love of God.

While family dynamics contribute to shaping how we view ourselves, others, and God, the truth is that we cannot prevent another's actions, nor blame them for our own internal responses and perceptions. We cannot blame them for the lies that Satan, *and our flesh*, speak to us in those moments, and which we choose to believe.

Abba Father wants us to work through family relationship issues with His love. However, sometimes that is not possible, even if we want it to be so. Thus, the place that first needs healing isn't in what happened, but the response within *us*. Abba Father wants to heal every *heart* wound through His love and truth that are able to tear down speculations and imaginations and lift us up into the realm of victorious perspectives.

The love of God isn't just tender, it is also *violent*. Truth and love rend dark veils so we can see God, and in seeing, be changed. Seeing Him is key to our wholeness—we become like Him as we *behold* Him (2 Cor. 3:18). If we gaze on the darkness of some offense, we become filled with offense. Playing it over and over in our mind with angry, bitter thoughts tears away peace and soundness from our soul. God wants our gaze on Him.

Not long ago I was in prayer and I remembered an incident that happened when I was about four years old. I was sitting on my father's lap and looking up into his eyes I said, "Daddy, I just don't know what to do." A family issue was pressing on my little mind and I needed dad to tell me how to deal with it. So too, God, as a Father, wants us to feel His embrace as we ask for His counsel regarding the daily events of life. As little children longing for

50

love, we seek approval from those around us. But when faced with loveless actions, we become confused and may not discern the secret lies forming within us. We disconnect and repress what we have no answer for.

We look for ways to escape circumstances, because we don't know how to face them with healthy solutions. No one has taught us how to climb onto Abba Father's lap. We wall our hearts to escape the pain, not realizing we are actually walling *in* the pain. We don't know how to open our heart to God, so we look for love through any means we think will meet our unmet needs. However, fellowship with God who is Light and Love will change all this.

God's restoration in our life is a continual work; He sees what we cannot see. Life with Him is a brilliant journey of ever *unfolding revelation* of Himself and who we are in Christ. The revelations of Himself that He gives us are to launch us into wider realms of freedom with authority to live as He intends. As Daniel 11:32 says, *"Those who know their God will display strength and take action."*

A PARENT'S OWN FRAMEWORK

Children are vulnerable and are completely dependent on another's care for them. But sometimes the one caring for them is operating out of their own unhealed wounds.

A parent's own response system is influenced by their own early family dynamics and perceptions. Their point of reference has also been shaped by personal experiences (good and bad), role models (good and bad), and types of support systems (or lack of them). They, like we, are also influenced by the spirit realm (good and bad). Many of our parents are on their own journey of being healed. Some have walked in wholeness much of their life. Some are still lost at sea waiting to be rescued.

Unmet needs can be expressed in many ways, including depression, anger, anxiety, isolating, and rebellion. It is also expressed through addictions. In truth, the list is endless.

While family wounds can leave us with a deep sense of unmet need, there are other harmful influences that also shape our thinking. These include certain cultural or religious customs that work to destroy a healthy family unit. In some cultures boys are esteemed and girls are not, women are shrouded or hidden away, or fathers sell their children to sex slave-traders.

Other cultures allow the killing of unwanted baby girls as an accepted practice. Societies that practice abortion promote a cultural mindset that approves the death of another's life for purposes of self-convenience. Whether intentional or not, unhealthy family behavior is often promoted through television programming where disrespect, verbal abuse, or physical violence are seen as a norm.

A child's thinking can be influenced by *many* sources including a child's own *mis*perceptions. Even the best parental skill cannot always prevent negative things from happening to a child, nor control a child's internal processing. Spiritual influences such as generational bondages are also another dynamic that may be at work in a parent's life—an influence that many may not be aware of, but may be influencing negative behavior. While the power of the curse is broken at the cross, continued personal sin or even a lack of taking authority over the wiles of the enemy, can give place for bondages to operate in one's life and thinking.

WHEN FATHERS ARE ABSENT

Statistics show that strong fathering helps children do better in school, be more confident, and be more successful in relationships. Studies also show that fathers who are involved with their children provide practical support and serve as models for their children's development.

Some may think it's primarily the son who needs a father to guide and instruct him, but a daughter also needs a father just as a son does. She needs a father who will teach her and give her a visual role model of what a man of integrity is like, and how she is to keep herself pure for marriage. A father prepares both a son and daughter for success in life.

Studies reveal that children of fatherless families have greater tendency toward early sexual activity, anxiety, poor educational performance, and increased demonstration of aggressive, uncoop-erative or antisocial behavior. They are also more likely to suffer child abuse or early death.[2]

Please note, these are just statistics and do not define a person's behavior simply because a father may not be present for any number of reasons.

According to US data, the presence of fathers has significant impact in the home, and so does their absence:

- 43% of US children live without their father [US Depart-ment of Census]
- 90% of homeless and runaway children are from fatherless homes. [US D.H.H.S., Bureau of the Census]
- 80% of rapists motivated with displaced anger come from fatherless homes. [Criminal Justice & Behavior, Vol. 14, pp. 403-26, 1978]
- 71% of pregnant teenagers lack a father. [U.S. Department of Health and Human Services press release, Friday, March 26, 1999]
- 63% of youth suicides are from fatherless homes. [US D.H.H.S., Bureau of the Census]
- 85% of children who exhibit behavioral disorders come from fatherless homes. [Center for Disease Control]
- 90% of adolescent repeat arsonists live with only their mother. [Wray Herbert, "Dousing the Kindlers," Psycholo-gy Today, January, 1985, p. 28]
- 71% of high school dropouts come from fatherless homes. [National Principals Association Report on the State of High Schools]
- 75% of adolescent patients in chemical abuse centers come from fatherless homes. [Rainbows for all God's Children]

- 70% of juveniles in state operated institutions have no father at home. [US Department of Justice, Special Report, Sept. 1988]
- 85% of youths in prisons grew up in a fatherless home. [Fulton County Georgia jail populations, Texas Department of Corrections, 1992]
- Fatherless boys and girls are: twice as likely to drop out of high school; twice as likely to end up in jail; four times more likely to need help for emotional or behavioral problems. [US D.H.H.S. news release, March 26, 1999] [3]
- Fathers are more likely to be the protector of the child: a British study found that children are 33 times more likely to be abused by a live-in boyfriend or stepfather. [4]
- The U.S. Department of Health and Human Services states that there were more than 1 million documented child abuse cases in 1990. In 1983, it found that 60% of perpetrators were women with sole custody. Shared parenting can significantly reduce the stress associated with sole custody, and reduce the isolation of children in abusive situations by allowing both parents to monitor the children's health and welfare and to protect them. [5]

These statistics reveal that children from fatherless homes are:
- 5 times more likely to commit suicide
- 32 times more likely to run away
- 20 times more likely to have behavioral disorders
- 14 times more likely to commit rape
- 9 times more likely to drop out of high school
- 20 times more likely to end up in prison [6]

Fatherlessness is expressed not only as the absence of a father, but when a father who is present does not, or *cannot*, provide for, or guide a child, whether through ignorance, inability, or even illness. Reasons for fatherlessness include: death, job situation, divorce, lack of commitment, believing that children are the "wife's responsibility," priority on materialism, drug use, affairs, rejection of conventional roles, and a parent's personal problems. Nonresident dads may keep involved in their children's lives, but often end up in a role more as a close relative rather than a father giving guidance and counsel. All these can greatly impact a child's full emotional growth.

Some people create their own "fatherlessness" by rejecting their parents and authorities, perhaps because of painful experiences. But we need fathers. We need Abba Father. Our wholeness and destiny depends on His presence. God never left us; it is we who have wandered from Him. And so He calls to us with open arms, calling us to return to His fathering care.

BREAKING FREE FROM A "FATHERLESS" MINDSET

God's truth sets us free, and freedom brings change. Some prefer to continue in blame, and disconnecting is sometimes easier than connecting. Sometimes its easier to be angry, kick the dog, yell at our spouse, throw tantrums, hit the kids, buy the bottle, and so on. Sometimes we'd rather coddle our agreement with an area of "struggle" rather than lose that "familiar friend" means of coping. Sometimes it's easier to put on a pretty face and say, "Everything is fine." But denial destroys the life we are meant to live and the divine intentions we are designed to experience. God wants to restore the broken areas in our hearts and heal the broken places within us.

Even Jesus wasn't a stranger to cruel words hurled at Him when ignorantly called a "bastard child," or when His brothers thought He was crazy doing ministry, or when His earthly step-dad died when Jesus was still young. The Son of Man wasn't sheltered from temptation, or hidden from the hostility of men. He was, however, a man of faith, joy, power, and authority because He lived in the bond of love with His Father.

Whether the family dynamics in which we grew up were wonderful, terrible, or somewhere in-between, we *can* walk in wholeness. We can have the same family framework with God that Jesus knew on this earth—we too can experience God's nearness and know our worth and value to Him who is our Abba Father.

Experiencing Abba Father's love for us will root us and ground us in the intimate knowledge that He is deeply involved with us as a Father, and not perhaps as how an earthly father may have been with us. Living from God's family framework will empower our heart to trust the leading of the Holy Spirit with confidence that He is not emotionally unsafe or overbearing as perhaps a mother may have been. The family framework of God will help us to see Jesus as Abba's Firstborn—our Brother—who treats us with absolute love and respect, and not as how an earthly brother may have taunted, abused, or ignored us.

In God's family every one of us is celebrated and valued as an important member of His family. We are loved and we love.

Our Father knows our needs and He sees our destiny. He wants to parent us in wholeness *and* for the divine purpose to which we have been called. There is healing in Abba's unfaltering love, and a purpose to the privilege of being born into His family.

Have You Been Born Into God's Family?

It's time to shed the fatherlessness that has kept us in the darkness of powerlessness and "orphan" thinking. It's time for a new framework and a new way of living. We have a dynamic, divine purpose to fulfill, and a life of love and authority to experience with God as our Father. For this, we must be born again.

Being *born of God* is a supernatural act of God. We have been born of the flesh *by* human flesh, but being born of God is *by* His Holy Spirit. We come to Jesus, just as we are, and receive Him; we receive the Spirit of the Son to become sons. The Son will reveal the Father to us. This is Abba Father's will for every one (1 Tim. 2:4).

Romans 10:8-10 says that if we *confess with our mouth* that Jesus is Lord, and *believe in our heart* that God raised Him from the dead, we will be saved. In God's world, believing is not a mere mental acknowledgement, it is the continual action of faith that listens and obeys. 1 John 1:9 says that if we confess our sins, God is faithful and just to forgive our sins and cleanse us from all unrighteousness.

Scripture says we are to take words with us and return to the Lord (Hos. 14:1-2). God responds to our words—words that come from our heart (Dan. 10:12).

Have you returned to the Father through the living pathway of the Son? If not, will you turn, believe, and follow Jesus now who is the Way to knowing Abba Father? If so, pray the following aloud:

Heavenly Father, You are the Father of all creation and are worthy to be honored. I confess that I have sinned and have lived my own way. I repent—I turn from sin and receive Your forgiveness through the blood of Your Son, Jesus, that was poured out on the cross to break the power of sin and death over me, and in me. I break agreement with Satan and I take the hand of Jesus and come into the Kingdom of light in Christ. I declare my faith that Jesus rose from the dead and is now seated in heaven with You, Father. I declare my faith in Christ, that through Him, I, too, can live in resurrection power of the Spirit. I receive you, Jesus, as my Lord and Savior. I give You my heart, soul, mind, and body—all that I am and have—I pick up my cross of sacrifice to follow You. I turn from a life of sin and independence, and I receive Your rightful place of counsel and guidance in my life, Father. I choose to live a life that honors You through relationship with You. Fill me and baptize me with Your Holy Spirit according to Your Word. Thank You, Father, for Your love and mercy. Thank You for a restored identity in You as Your child. In Jesus' name, Amen.

Such a confession is only the beginning of a new life as you turn your course to follow Christ whole-heartedly and continually. When you are born again by the Spirit of God, He gives you His transforming power to become a living son of God—a growth process of development in faith, truth, and love through the Spirit of grace.

When you are born of God, did you know that the angels rejoice over you? They rejoice over every child of God born of His Spirit (Luke 15:10). You are celebrated by God and all of heaven as they throw a new-birth celebration just for you. They are extremely glad you were born. Your life causes heaven to sing for joy!

Heavenly Father, thank You for Your salvation in Christ! Thank You that we are no longer orphans in this world, but we have a new Family— the Family of God.

PERSONAL APPLICATION:

1. What was your parent's personal "framework" like?
2. How do you view yourself? Valuable? Wanted? Loved? Loving?
3. Do you see any stronghold in your thinking?
4. Have you made any negative judgment or vow regarding another person? What was it?
5. Have you broken agreement with that judgment and vow?
6. Have you been born again? What was your experience like?

CHAPTER 4

HEALING THE WOUNDED HEART

"When my father and my mother forsake me,
then the LORD will take me up." — King David [1]

We have glimpsed the foundations that God has placed in humanity regarding a father's role. We've also seen how sin has created brokenness in human relationships, yet how God has a framework for our healing in knowing Him as our Abba Father.

Though an earthly family may sometimes fail us, and we them, God never fails us. He wants to stop the pain *and* the darkness that promotes a continued affliction in our heart. Some wounds go very deep and the crippling effect can last a lifetime if not addressed. The truth is that we often don't know what to do with the pain we feel but cannot physically see. Some people ignore or "stuff" the pain of past events while others build walls or hide in addictions. Others look for help. Not dealing with lingering issues, however, only holds us captive to the pain of the past.

The evidence of unhealed emotional wounds reminds me of what I saw at Pearl Harbor one time when on vacation with our family. At the bottom of Pearl Harbor in Oahu, Hawaii, lies a naval ship—the *U.S.S. Arizona*. The U.S. battleship was sunk in the Japanese Naval attack on Pearl Harbor in December, 1941. Today, oil from within the ship continues to seep in tiny quantities that rise to the surface of the harbor where the ship lies. They call these seepages the "tears" of the 1177 men who died inside the *Arizona's* sunken hull.

The "tears" of oil are the evidence of what is still trapped beneath.

What rises to the top of our thoughts and emotions in stressful circumstances? Do we have "tears" that rise when our "buttons" get pushed? Are there unresolved issues that linger beneath the surface as we go about our routine life?

Unhealed pain *will* come out in one way or another—whether through troubled relationships, inability to draw near to God, or constant feelings of anger, guilt, or shame. It might manifest as self-sabotaging behavior, or a plaguing sense of personal "unworthiness." Our "tears" may rise as anxiety, withdrawal, rage, or perhaps in conversation as an off-handed comment laced with an underlying negative meaning.

Unloving actions by others toward us can never be justified, but neither are we to remain in the lies or bitterness inspired by those actions. If we stay captive to the past, we will not move forward into the full purposes that Abba Father has uniquely designed for our life. Time is short and our life too valuable to waste in the failures of yesterday—ours or anybody else's.

We can't change the past or what other people chose to say and do, including a family member. We can only choose *personal* change by coming to the Great Physician's healing room—the cross. The cross breaks the tyranny of loveless lies that enthrone themselves in our mind and emotions. Only when we bring our heart and mind to the light of love, can we rise to a new life of triumph. And for this to happen, *I* must be crucified (Gal. 2:20).

At the cross, we find healing for the whole man. Healing is often a process, especially for the wounded heart and soul, but it is real and it is available. Four special keys that Jesus has taught me in my own healing process are: truth, forgiveness, the way of love, and engaging a lifestyle of honor.

1 HEALING THROUGH TRUTH

Jesus said, ". . . I am the way, and the truth, and the life;
no one comes to the Father but through Me." (John 14:6)

Our Father sent Jesus to us; He is Truth Incarnate and the Great Physician who heals our spirit, soul, and body. He is the Door that brings us into Father's healing room (John 10:9). For any healing to take place, we must come out of hiding, denial, and pretending the problem doesn't exist. We have to be honest about our need. As we present our heart to Jesus, He will remove the thorns that pierced our heart and cleanse the infection that has filled our mind (Ps. 20:6; 21:8).

When Jesus wore a *crown of thorns* on the cross, it symbolized taking upon Himself the dominion of our fallen mindsets and the strongholds that have held our thoughts captive to brokenness, and one of those places of captivity is the "fatherless" mindset. **The bleeding hands, feet, and side of Incarnate Truth not only condemned sin and lawlessness, but the vile lies that we are unloved, unvalued, and alone.**

Divine Truth is the healing antidote to the paralyzing poison of the devil's deceptions and his lies about God and who we are. Satan employs *falsehoods* to deplete us of love, power, and a sound mind, but truth restores us to empowered living through intimacy with God's love. Satan's lies kill the delight in who we are as humans made in God's likeness as precious, valuable and having great purpose. Like a python snake, Satan's cunning words seek our agreement in order to choke off our engagement with the Father's voice, and in so doing, cut off our life and destiny.

The framework of self too often glues our gaze on failures—ours, others and things we cannot change. It rehearses over and over a personal loss or injury. But this ungodly gaze ignores God and neglects the state of our own heart, and as they say, two wrongs don't make a right. Truth returns our gaze to see Hope and Love and makes our heart right with clear thinking for right action.

Jesus said that by *abiding in truth*, the truth would set us free (John 8:31-32). **Truth magnifies God as greater than human failures and circumstances.** It sees Father's love and hears His counsel in the midst of our tragedies, and trusts Him to bring something good out of it all (Rom. 8:28). Lies lead us into self-destructive ways, but truth leads us into life and liberty.

Truth is found in fellowship with God and His Word (John 17:17). Truth is revealed to us by the Spirit of Truth—the Holy Spirit. God is truth and His children are a family of truth (Zech. 8:3). Truth gives us divine perspective (versus human reasoning) and restores us to right thinking. When we believe the truth that God is near, that is how we'll respond to life. If we believe we need His approval alone, we won't drown in the rejection of others. If we believe He has a divine plan for our lives, we won't try to figure things out on our own. If we believe He loves mankind, that is how we'll perceive others, even those who have hurt us. And if we believe we are His beloved and are not "abusable," we will live with right boundaries knowing our authority in Christ.

We come to truth through the cross—coming on bended knee. Psalm 139:23-24 says that we come to God *humbly,* asking Him to search *our* hearts to see what hurtful ways are in *us.* A *proud* heart refuses healing, because healing requires the laying down of self. Pride says, "I know better than God." **It is a "Father-rejecting" mindset and heart.** But Jesus said that His sheep hear His voice and follow Him, and He leads us to resurrection life through the cross (John 10:27). There at the cross we learn to recognize and renounce lies and sin in the light of truth. This brings healing.

2 HEALING THROUGH FORGIVENESS

The *natural* response of our flesh is to hurt those who hurt us. We want retribution, revenge, and justice! What they did was unfair, unkind, insensitive, and cruel. We want them to pay for how they've hurt us, or maybe someone we love. We want them to feel sorry for what they've done and the pain they've inflicted through their actions, or even through their absence.

The fundamental nature of an offense is rooted in a broken law of love. A broken law demands justice. However, vengeful, self-centered responses (whether in action or attitude) can never repair what was broken. We cannot change the past, nor can justice be served on the platter of unforgiveness.

Father is a just Father, but His ways are not our ways and He *will* make all things right in His time and His way. He does not condone wrong doing, but to heal us fully He *requires* us to forgive others just as He forgives us. In fact, we must forgive others to receive His forgiveness.

Forgiveness chooses to *trust* God's fathering care in our life as He works all things for good. It chooses to *trust* Father to work out *His* own plan in another's life.

Jesus taught four important principles regarding forgiveness:

- Forgiveness is released to us *when* we forgive those who sin against us (Matt. 6:12)
- If we do not forgive others, Father will not forgive us (Matt. 6:15)
- We are judged in the same way we judge others (Matt. 7:2)
- We are to forgive unconditionally (Matt. 18:22)

Forgiving others opens the portal of Father's forgiveness so that we can *experience* His forgiveness and nearness that ministers to our *deepest* need. Unforgiveness, however, is a place of torment—not for the other person—but for us. When we continually replay the events of the past and rehearse resentment, we hold *ourselves* captive to the past. When we deliberately ignore someone and think about how we can withhold good things from them, we are inviting darkness to dwell in us.

Bitterness in the heart distorts our perceptions of everything and causes us to see the world—past, present, and future—through a dark filter of personal woe. God created us to live in joyful expectation, not woe. A world of woe is self-focused. It is a Fatherless world.

Some people forgive readily, others with difficulty—perhaps because of the nature of the offense (or offenses), or the depth of grief involved. Some say it is impossible and the offense unforgiveable. But our healing *cannot* come until we are willing to give up our control of circumstances *and* others, and forgive.

Unforgiveness is a lie that makes us feel we have a special power over the other person, but in reality it drains us of power as it eats away joy, hindering fellowship with God and others. Unforgiveness holds our emotions in a snare of endless grief, depression, or anger, pillaging the peace of our soul over things we cannot change, and holding us in a loveless place.

That family member who broke the law of love did so because of a multitude of reasons. We may never know the depths of why, but Father God does. Every one of us can be so lost in our own world of pain and unmet needs that we don't realize the hurt we *commit*, or love we *omit*. The ones who have hurt us may not know, or unfortunately, may not care—or have the ability to care. But God cares, and the bottom line is that we live our life before Him, in Him, and through Him. Only when we give the situation to Him can healing mend our heart where earthly families and significant relationships in our lives fail.

The cross replaces human reasoning with *divine* perspective. It removes our false sense of self-justification and enables us to see ourselves, and others, through the Father's eyes.

To drink from the cup of healing, our hand must let go of the offense. As we do, our hand is free to grasp Abba's hand as He pulls us up and into His arms where He imparts the love and value our family may have been unable to give us. His love heals the *root* of our pain while removing any feeling of inferiority or shame. Forgiveness brings closure to the open-ended cycle of inward suffering as we release that individual into the Father's hands.

As Son of Man, Jesus was unmercifully beaten and crucified, yet He forgave those who beat Him. He didn't wait for them to ask His forgiveness for what they were doing; He didn't wait for them to say, "I'm sorry." He said, *"Father, forgive them, for they know not what they do"* (Luke 23:34).

At the cross, Jesus gives us a different perspective when others act cruelly. His love empowers us to forgive others of their *loveless* crimes. Jesus Himself was not *above* the pain of the cross. He felt it all—outwardly and inwardly. Not only was His body beaten, but He experienced the download of *all* the sin and infirmity of *all* mankind upon Himself, including yours and mine.

Think about that for a moment. Jesus experienced every hurt we have ever received *and* the hurt we have inflicted on others, whether through commission or omission. On the cross, Jesus experienced the full cup of our sin; He experienced our dark mindsets and ugly response systems—taking them all upon Himself. He did this to secure our forgiveness and our freedom. And look at what the Father did with Jesus' sacrifice—He turned the evil (man's cruel actions) inflicted on Jesus to become a blessing for the whole world. Jesus' blood and suffering became the payment for our redemption as He forgave those who nailed Him to the cross, and committed Himself into Abba's hands.

Abba Father has promised that all things work together for good to those who love Him and are called according to His purpose (Rom. 8:28). Anything we have ever gone through and have given into our Heavenly Father's hands, He can turn to be a blessing. Just trust Him.

As we commit our lives to our Abba Father, even our negative events can become catalysts for something good through His hands. The opposite is true as well: when we do *not* commit ourselves to the Father in the midst of painful circumstances, our own responses can become agents of further destruction in our life and to those around us. I have heard it said more than once that it is not what happens *to* us, but what happens *in* us that shapes our life most. I have personally found that statement to be true.

STEPPING OUTSIDE THE BLAME BOX

As bitter roots are exposed, the act of forgiveness *uproots* them from continuing to ensnare our heart, breaking the controlling

65

mandates of self. When Jesus said to forgive seventy times seven, He didn't mean we are to count the number of offenses, but that we should forgive *always*! Such forgiveness means we take off our black robes of judgment, repent of vows we've made, and renounce the deception that tells us we have the right to be another's judge and jury. God alone has that place, and He says, "Judge not lest you be judged" (Matt. 7:1). There are, however, judgments that God *does* want us to make regarding spirits and their fruit in our lives. Remember, in Christ we are the body of the Righteous Judge.

When we forgive others, we honor the Father who tells us to do so. When we take responsibility for our own attitudes, it frees us from living with a "victim" mentality. When finger-pointing is replaced with uplifted hands of worship, power is restored to our life. Our flesh will hesitate, but it is a choice that brings healing.

The truth is that we cannot control another person's actions or demand they make right choices; we can only be accountable for our own responses. When we remove our stranglehold from the neck of another, we free Father's hands to deal with them in His time and *His* way. His way always seeks redemption...this is what He has done for us. It is not that we condone a wrongful event, or justify the wrong, but that we put justice in Father's hands and let Him direct our action. His justice is accurate—ours is not.

BOUNDARIES VERSUS WALLS

When we feel hurt by others the natural mind may say, "I'm going to build a wall around me and no one is coming in unless I say so!" We want protection so we pull back, isolate, slam the door and put out our guard dogs. But self-protecting walls are self-defeating by nature because they operate by a *spirit of offense* and *fear*. Anything done through agreement with offense and fear will work death in us. There may be times when we *do* need literal protection and we may need to notify an authority. This is not having a "wall," but having a right boundary.

Its okay to tell someone "no" when we do not want them to cross lines with us. This promotes inward confidence and better relationships. Father wants us to relate to one another with *right boundaries.* The important thing to discern is if we are operating in offense and fear, or in truth and love through right boundaries rather than walls.

FORGIVING OURSELVES

Family members, leaders, and others are not the only ones we need to forgive. When God says to forgive, it means forgiving ourselves, too. This means *freeing ourselves* from self-imposed judgments and vows. Self-condemnation is ungodly thinking and is a loveless act that we must also surrender at the cross.

Satan is the accuser of the brethren and we must not join him to tear ourselves down, to punish ourselves for past failures. This does not please our Abba Father who sent His Son to set us free. Keeping ourselves "behind bars" in unforgiveness robs us of joy, peace, and strength. It denies the cleansing power of Christ's blood. This means it also robs Father of the fruit of our gifts and purpose for which we are called, because when we are in captivity our gifts are too. If God has forgiven us, then choosing to not forgive ourselves is esteeming ourselves greater than Him, and our judgments superior to His redemption. This prevents healing.

GRUDGES AGAINST GOD

Sometimes we carry judgments against God for not preventing some harmful thing that happened, or not doing what we want Him to do. Anger is a part of the healing process of grief, but when we hold on to blame against God, it becomes a prison. Again, it holds us in a loveless place and out of fellowship with the very One we need the most—the only One who has the true answers we seek and cannot find within ourselves. Lingering grudges are rooted in pride and link with the accuser, Satan.

Someday we will have the answers to our myriad questions. But until then, a life of healing and power is released through trusting God with our issues. Our human mind doesn't have to understand everything, though we'd like to. Meanwhile, talk to Him about your situations, and trust Him.

3   HEALING THROUGH LOVE

We were created for love. Each one of us perceives the affirming of that love in different ways and through specific actions of others—actions that tell us whether we are loved, or not. The specific ways that love is perceived by our heart is often called our *"love language."* Wounds within family are deepest when they impact our love language, whether through abuse or neglect. Fathers and family are, after all, the most significant people in our lives.

Knowing we are loved and affirmed is important. Even Abba Father affirmed His Son, Jesus (Matt. 3:17). Author Gary Chapman has written a series of books on what he says are people's top five "love languages." [2] He lists them as:

- Words of affirmation
- Physical touch
- Quality time
- Acts of service
- Gifts

Here are some examples of how these languages work. When our love language is ***words of affirmation***, we feel loved by receiving encouraging words. When it is ***physical touch***, we feel affirmed through hugs and pats on the back. When our love language is ***quality time***, we feel valued when someone takes time with us. When our language is ***acts of service***, we feel loved when another takes time to help us with things. And when our love language is ***gifts***, we feel valued when someone gives us something simply because they want to show us we are loved.

The opposite speaks another message to us, as well. *Abuse,* or *neglect* in the area of our personal love language can convey an impression that we are not loved or valued. For example, verbal abuse, as well as the *absence* of encouraging words, can make us feel unloved; physical abuse or the absence of hugs and pats on the back can make us feel unvalued; a parent who is too busy for us can make us feel we are not *worth* their time; a parent who is never there to help us, or never thinks about giving us something as a tangible expression of our value to them, can make us feel unnoticed or unloved. And too, using any of the love languages as a way to manipulate us is an abuse of that language, such as the giving of gifts as a way to compensate for one's absence.

The sense of being unloved can make us feel depressed and angry, and is a root cause of many behavioral issues in children and young people, including suicide. If our parent's own love language was abused or neglected in their own formative years, and they have not found healing, their actions toward us will generally spring from their own sense of feeling unloved, unvalued, or not validated. And too, our parent's own love language may be different than our own, and any neglect may have been purely unintentional.

A life of power is one that is rooted and grounded in love (Eph. 3:17; Rom. 5:5). Abba Father has healing for each one of us in our own particular "love language." No matter what our love language is, the Father, Son, and Holy Spirit manifest love to us in *every possible way*! Let's look.

Words of affirmation: God affirms us through His Word. Read it! Ask the Holy Spirit to reveal its truths to you. It is full of His passion and affirmation of who you are to Him. You are His beloved. Some people say they read the Bible and all they see is condemnation and judgment. This may be due to a wrong lens through which they are reading it, or false teaching.

God shows His loving affirmation of us by speaking to us—to our inner man. We may know His voice as a "still small voice." He also speaks to us through others, through dreams, thoughts, and myriad other ways (more on this in Chapter 8). The more we intimately know His love and affirmation, we won't drown in the rejection experienced from another.

Touch: God touches our life through His manifest presence. As we learn to know Him, we learn to recognize the expressions of His activity in us, with us, and around us. We may express an encounter we have with Him by saying, "He touched me," or "He touched my heart." Father also sends people to minister to us the tangible touch of His love through hugs and physical expressions of encouragement. He is not limited!

Quality time: The Father, Son, and Holy Spirit love quality time with us. When we set apart time for prayer, worship, and meditation in His Word, He will come and make Himself known to us. He has promised that if we draw near to Him, He *will* draw near to us (James 4:8). In those moments of just being with Him, we will experience His presence renewing our strength, opening our understanding, and learning from Him about what He is doing, *and* our participation with Him in His activities on earth.

Acts of service: The cross was the greatest act of service ever given us by Abba Father. And yet, He continues to express His love through acts of service by sending us help and provision in myriad ways, too numerous to count, on a daily basis—both through supernatural and natural means. Sometimes we just need to stop and thank God for all the things that He *has* done for us, rather than whining about what He *hasn't* done. Gratitude helps us to see the abundance of His active goodness towards us.

Gifts: Abba Father lavishes us with gifts. The *greatest* gifts He ever gave us was the gift of His Son and the indwelling presence of His Holy Spirit (John 4:10; Luke 11:13). More gifts from God are expressed in many ways—every good thing that comes our way is a gift from Him. Every talent, ability, and call is a gift not just *for* us, but to us *for* others.

The Father, Son, and Holy Spirit each have specific *spiritual* gifts for us.

- Romans 12 shows us a list of **gifts from Father**: prophecy, service, teaching, encouragement, giving, leadership, and the gift of mercy.
- 1 Corinthians 12 gives us a list of **gifts from the Holy Spirit**: word of wisdom, word of knowledge, gift of faith, gifts

of healing, miracles, prophecy, discerning of spirits, tongues, and interpretation of tongues.

- Ephesians 4 shows a list of **gifts from Jesus**: apostles, prophets, evangelists, pastors and teachers.

RECEIVING AND RELEASING LOVE

While God is able to fill every unmet need, the greatest healing power of God's love can only be *fully* experienced by giving what we receive.

God's love is a river that heals *as* it flows. That is why one of the biggest hindrances to healing is self-pity. Self-pity is like a clog in a pipe that stops the flow of living waters. Self-pity is a "victim" mindset—a hand that takes and forgets to give. Self-pity enflames the feelings of being unloved because it is self-seeking, operating like a "black hole" that draws everything inward and is never satisfied.

1 Corinthians 13 says that *love is not self-seeking, self-serving or self-exalting*. Healing doesn't come by pulling on others to love us, and hoping they will affirm us. It happens when we become God-centered rather than self-centered, then love will flow.

When we seek to love others, the movement of God's love through us will automatically make us feel loved, too, as we experience His love for them. While we typically give love in the way we like to receive it, it's helpful to learn others' love languages so that we can speak to them in their "language."

Abba Father wants to not only affirm His love to us, but affirm His love to others through our words and actions. **When we *give* His love, we feel His love! When we feel His love, we feel whole.**

God is love and His gifts express His love, not just to us, but in loving service through us to others. Gifts are not meant to be self-gratifying or self-promoting because love is not self-serving. God's gifts are His way of blessing us by blessing others *through* us! They are not given to exalt our own name, but our Father's name as we serve others and advance His Kingdom.

71

God's Word teaches that the *greatest* pursuit in life should be to love, and that without it, we are nothing (1 Cor. 13:1). To pursue love is to seek His nature to fill our every thought, action, word, and motive in every circumstance.

"Love is patient, love is kind, and is not jealous;
love does not brag, and is not arrogant, does not act unbecomingly; it
does not seek its own, is not provoked, does not take into account a
wrong suffered, does not rejoice in unrighteousness, but rejoices with the
truth; bears all things, believes all things, hopes all things, endures all
things. Love never fails..." 1 Corinthians 13:4-7

4 HEALING THROUGH HONOR

Many people do not realize the power of honor, but God says that honor releases the promise of blessing and wellbeing. Of the Ten Commandments that God gave to Moses, the command for children to honor their parents was the only one accompanied by a promise.

"Honor your father and your mother as the Lord your God
has commanded you, that your days may be prolonged and that it
may go well with you on the land which the
Lord your God gives you." Deuteronomy 5:16

When we choose to *be* honorable toward parents, we release the promise of God to bless us with wellbeing and a full destiny. The opposite is also true—*dishonor* of parents reaps destruction and cuts off divine blessing (Deut. 21:20-21). Honor reaps honor. Dishonor reaps dishonor.

The word *"honor"* (Heb. *"kabad"*) means: "public esteem, reverence, and recognition of the right of someone who has a *superior standing.*" Honor is an attitude of esteem with accompanying actions. The Hebrew word for *"honor"* is a derivative of the word *"glory"* (*kabowd*)—a term used to describe the majestic splendor of God's attributes and presence. Honor is linked to God's glory.

Respecting parents and seeking to bring them honor is an attitude of humility; it acknowledges those who gave us life as being greater than ourselves, no matter what they have done. It cuts to the heart of self-centeredness because honor involves the laying down of *self*. It forms within us a framework that our life is not about ourselves.

Parents, of all people, should be honored because they are the very reason for our existence. This, in itself, signifies a position of being *greater than ourselves*. We honor them not because of what they do, or don't do, but because of their position. Honoring them honors God, and makes us *honorable*.

I realize that because of a parent's harshness or sin, some say they cannot honor those who have hurt them or abandoned them. But honor isn't about the other person's behavior, but about *our own* attitude. Our parents are held accountable to God for their actions, just as we also are held accountable for ours. Abba Father wants to heal our wounds and teach us true honor.

Please understand that honoring parents does *not* mean willing obedience to an activity they may demand of us that is contrary to God's Word. Many lives have been deeply wounded through ungodly parental demands with vulnerable children. The honor that God teaches is respect through love, not obedience to evil or honor through fear that carries torment.

Some leaders use fear to command obedience, but such actions dishonor the highest authority—God, for God is the One who gives authority and His authority is to operate through love. To abuse a position of authority is to dishonor God. While we obey what is right and just with honorable actions, we also do not compromise with what is unrighteous.

Jesus was the most whole person on earth and He lived a lifestyle of honor; He never responded in fear or catered to a person's manipulative and sinful nature. He didn't given in to intimidation, but was humble and obedient to His Father. He respected people, but He also firmly addressed *spiritual* leaders' abuse of power and any dishonor of the Father.

73

Jesus honored Abba and brought Him glory, rather than glorifying Himself. The cross was the ultimate act of honor as He laid down His life for the Father's will to be done. That act of honor released healing to all mankind.

Our attitudes of honor release healing not only in us, but into our sphere of influence. I myself am still walking out some healing from certain family wounds—mostly from my mother who is now in heaven. Wounds I experienced in our relationship still rise, now and then, like those "tears" of the *U.S.S. Arizona*. I have learned to continue the healing process by thanking God for her and remembering the good, for there *was* good, much good. I look for opportunities to honor her, sometimes in ways that only God knows, and that she sees as she watches over me together with the cloud of witnesses that surround us. And most of all, I know. And it is building in me a heart of honor that influences everything else in my life.

FREE FROM THE PAIN OF THE PAST

No matter what our past has been, there is healing in the Father's love. He has provided for our full healing, restoration, and the fulfillment of every need. Our wonderful Shepherd and Brother calls us to pick up our cross and follow Him—He extends His hand for us to grasp and walk with Him into wholeness through truth, forgiveness, love, and honor as Abba's cherished child.

PERSONAL APPLICATION:

1. **Ask Holy Spirit to search your heart**. What does the Father want you to break agreement with? As Holy Spirit shows you, ask Father to wash you completely. Example: *"Father, show me Your heart, and my own. Holy Spirit, show me the truth. Father, I acknowledge my sin. I ask You to forgive me of (name sin). I break agreement with it right now. I renounce the lie that (name the lie that you have believed). I break agreement*

with it and I command every spirit that has come in through that lie and my agreement with it, to go now from me. I ask You, Jesus to wash me from all sin and disobedience. I declare the truth that <u>(speak the truth that He shows you)</u>. Father, fill me now with Your Holy Spirit as I surrender to You and follow Your leading completely from this day forward."

2. **Ask Jesus to show you anyone you need to forgive.** This includes family members or any other person, **including yourself.** Verbally declare: *"I forgive (name of individual) for (their words / actions). I let the offense go and I release them from my demands regarding it. I commit the situation into Your hands, Father. I ask that You would cleanse me from all resentment and I ask that You would bless them with the revelation of Yourself, even as You have revealed Yourself to me."* (Read: Matthew 7:1-5, 12; Colossians 3:13; Matthew 18:21-35)

3. **Ask Father to show you any walls you may have erected,** and what that wall is. Ask Him to hold you as you give Him permission to take down the false-security around your heart. Ask Him what He is going to replace that wall with—let Him show or speak to you what it is. You might get a picture, or word, or sense of what that is (i.e., His arms of love, His shield of favor, or maybe something else).

4. **Ask Father what judgment or vow you might have made** against a father or mother (Example: "My father didn't love me... I will never be like him." Or, "My parents were too strict... I will do what I want").

    Verbally declare: *"I renounce the unrighteous **judgment** that my father / mother _____. I renounce the **vow** that _____. I let the offense go and I bless them. Jesus, wash away all sin regarding this as I surrender fully to You."* (Read: John 8:15-16; 2 Corinthians 5:10; Romans 14:12-13)

5. **Ask Holy Spirit to fill you with God's love** as you declare gratitude and praise. Example: *"Holy Spirit, fill me with the Father's awesome love! As You wash away all sin and shame, replace them with peace and glory. I invite Your wisdom and grace into my life. I declare that I no longer have a spirit of fear, but I*

have a Spirit of love, power and a sound mind. I thank You that I am now filled with strength, hope, and courage as I yield to Your Spirit of holiness to change me. I thank You that I am blessed as I embrace a lifestyle of honor and humility. I discern Your love for me, Father, and I release that love to others, including those who have hurt me. Your goodness is with me continually. My heart will run after You that I might know You intimately, and make You known. In Jesus' name, Amen."

CHAPTER 5

YOU CAN CALL HIM "PAPA"

"For you have not received the spirit of bondage again to fear;
But you have received the Spirit of adoption,
Whereby we cry, 'Abba, Father.'"
—The Apostle Paul [1]

The healing of our heart from past wounds helps us to engage more fully the beautiful realities of God as a good, near, and involved parent. Everything we have and need comes from Abba Father. The Father sent the Son to redeem us and the Holy Spirit to lead us into the light of His love. Father is with us, watching over us, working with us, loving us.

The muddied filters through which we have viewed God and ourselves, formed from negative experiences with earthly families, are removed when we see our Father's pure love for us. False doctrines, worldly philosophies, and even some Church traditions (as well as plain ignorance) that have skewed our perception of Him will be seen for the lies they are when we step into the beautiful light of who He really is.

Our Father wants to be truly known and not judged by a false report we may have believed about Him. It's time to know the truth about our Abba Father. Only when we truly know Him will we truly know who we are.

We may readily see the Father as great, holy, exalted, and mighty, yet distant or indifferent to our personal needs. **Our theology may esteem Him as the omnipotent Heavenly Father, yet our heart never enter into a real experience of trusting and knowing Him as "*Dad*."**

Just as a healthy relationship with an earthly father grows and deepens through the years, so does a healthy relationship with God grow and deepen with experience. We are continually learning of who He is and who we are in Him and to Him.

I can mark the seasons in my life by the different revelations of God I've received as I've journeyed life with Him. Each fresh revelation brings breakthrough into a new place of intimacy and fellowship with Him. This enlarges my ability to walk and grow in divine purpose.

I came to Jesus through the revelation of my need for Him as my *Savior*. Inner freedom came when I began to know Him as my *Lord and Mighty Deliverer*. As I grew spiritually, Jesus revealed Himself to me as my *Bridegroom King*, captivating my heart as the *Lover of my soul*. I remember the season when the Holy Spirit revealed Himself to me as my *Teacher* and *Helper*. Other seasons have brought other revelations leading to deeper fellowship with God as my *Counselor, Potter, Shepherd, and Healer*. Then came the revelation of "*Abba Father*."

That revelation came after many years of ministry. The revelation came in response to an incident that triggered a deep emotional response in me. The details and background are lengthy, but suffice it to say that a flood of emotions that had been dammed up in me for years were loosed, and my soul was overwhelmed. Those flood waters were the words and negative actions of others—significant people in my past—that I had swept under the proverbial rug. I had practiced forgiving them in trying to keep my own heart right, but I didn't realize how much I had *internalized* the underlying message of their actions toward me.

While I was a deeply committed Christian, knowing I was loved by God, I was (unknowingly) believing someone else's loveless actions as the definition of my worth and value. My pastor, recognizing my distress, sent me to a Christian Counselor, even helping to pay for some of the fee. The first few counseling sessions were helpful in identifying and resolving some early family issues, along with a fresh release of forgiveness. But it was the last session that brought the deep healing I needed. It was an encounter with Abba Father, one that has anchored my life in a deep confidence in Him as His daughter. Like my moment of intimate encounter with Jesus, years prior in Argentina, this proved to be a deep life-transforming moment in God's presence. Only this time it was specifically with the Father.

The night before that last session, God gave me a dream. In the dream, the counselor and I were in the home where I grew up. We were there to do a counseling session. However, before the counseling could begin, he said we needed a keyboard as he felt music would be important to this session (remember, this was all in the dream). We entered my parent's house and began going through each room; we entered the family room first where we found my dad sitting in a chair. The room was a terrible mess! Stuff was thrown everywhere, chairs were overturned and drawers were pulled out. It was in total disarray. We continued through the house where we met each of my family members, each in different rooms, and each doing something that was typical to their personality and how I knew them growing up. That was the end of the dream.

The counselor and I discussed many of the elements in the dream and we knew it was from God. As we began to talk about my dad, the Holy Spirit prompted him to get up and put on a CD with a song about Abba Father. As the song played, a deep well in me burst open; I sat there and wept for well over an hour as the song played again and again.

In those moments, Abba Father revealed Himself to me in a way I had not known Him. I saw Him as my Heavenly Father who was not distant and unknowable, but as Abba who was pulling me up into His arms to comfort me. He was there for me, watching over me, holding me, feeling my pain, and affirming me.

79

It wasn't someone else ministering these things to me, it was directly Him to me as His daughter.

The truth is that my earthly father was a great dad who loved me deeply—I never doubted it. However, as in my dream, as a father he sometimes didn't know how to deal with the chaos our family experienced in life or in relationship with one another, as also reflected in the dream. In that encounter with Abba, God brought me into a deeper understanding that no matter what happens in my life, His Fathering care is ever present and He knows what to do. His wisdom is able to bring peace and order to the dysfunction I experience in this world. I don't have to fear. He has me covered when life seems out of control.

My earthly father passed away many years ago, and I cherish all the memories I have of him. I know he did the best he knew how with our family. I'm grateful that Abba Father is ever with us, even in the midst of our imperfections. He sees our weaknesses and never leaves us, but gives us His love and counsel. I'm grateful for His help with me as a parent where I fail, whether by actions committed or those omitted. I'm thankful for Abba's care that teaches me daily how to rightly relate to Him, myself, and others.

JESUS CALLED HIM ABBA FATHER

In the Old Testament, pictures of God's *fatherhood* were seen, but the term "Father" was not used when addressing Him. God's people felt that God Almighty was too holy to be addressed personally in such a familiar way—even though God called Himself a Father (Mal. 1:6). Nevertheless, the *understanding* of God's Fatherhood was there; the knowledge of God included both paternal and maternal care.

This was seen in the very names by which God revealed Himself to His people, such as: *"Jehovah-Jireh"* ("The Lord will **provide**"—Gen. 22:14), and *"El Shaddai"* (Almighty; God who is "the **many breasted One**"—Gen. 35:11—this name comes from the root word *"shadad"* meaning "to overcome" and is also connected to the Hebrew word *"shadayim"* which means "breasts, or what nurtures"). The name *El Shaddai* is linked to blessing and fruitfulness as He shows Himself to be the "One who is more than sufficient."

While God is understood to be a "Father" in the Old Testament, Jesus ushered in a whole new paradigm in which we not only see God as the Father, but know Him personally as our *Abba Father*. "Father" was Jesus' favorite term when praying or teaching about God, and the term is recorded sixty-five times in the synoptic gospels (Matthew, Mark, and Luke), and over one hundred times in the book of John. Paul's New Testament letters also describe God as "Father" over forty times. And yet, the whole Old Testament had referenced Him as a Father only fifteen times.[2]

Jesus modeled for us a daily life of fellowship with Abba Father. He was sent from the Father to remove everything that hinders us from knowing God as our "Abba." **Jesus taught that addressing God as "Abba" was not merely "*a*" way to address Him, but as "*the*" way to approach and know Him** (Mark 14:36). The apostle Paul also used this term, "Abba" (Rom. 8:15; Gal. 4:6).

As we learned earlier, *Abba* was an Aramaic word used by the Hebrews that was translated in other New Testament Scriptures by the Greek word *"Pater."* Again, the English equivalent is *"my father,"* and is a family term inferring a closeness such as how we might say *"Papa"* or *"Dad,"* though it is more than that. It is a family term of position used not only by children in speaking to their fathers, but also by adults when addressing a father with whom they had a close relationship.

Abba is a covenant term that conveys honor and loving respect. Calling God *"Abba Father"* infers both closeness and the honor of His sovereignty over our lives; it reflects His position of governing care for us, and our responsibility to Him as His heirs.

Jesus is the Firstborn among those who know God as Abba Father—as "Papa," in every reverential sense of the word. He is the First of a lineage of Kingdom heirs who do the Father's will on earth as it is in heaven. Even at twelve years of age, Jesus understood His position as the Son, and so He practiced a life yielded to the Father, allowing Abba to *father* Him in divine purpose.

This is the life that Jesus brings us into—one that is not only *born* of God, but is also *fathered* by Abba as His royal inheritance.

FATHERING IS ABOUT RELATIONSHIP

The very nature of fathering is relationship; it is training for destiny that is centered in a loving *bond* between a father and his child.

> *"And because you are sons, God has sent forth the Spirit of His Son into your hearts, crying Abba Father." —Galatians 4:6*

God is Spirit and not a man. The only way we can know God as Abba Father is by being born of His Spirit. Knowing God as *our Father (our Dad)* may not only be radical compared to the Old Testament, it may be radical to you. You may even think calling Him *"Dad"* or *"Papa"* is not holy enough. But again, the Aramaic term *"Abba"* is no more "holy" than similar English equivalents.

While reverence involves our words, true reverence goes beyond formalities. Reverence for Father is a matter of the heart. We all know what it is to outwardly address someone with honor, yet perhaps inwardly reject them. Too much of Church culture has done this very thing—God calls it "lip service," offering verbal honor while the heart is distant from Him. Jesus Himself joined with the voice of the Prophet Isaiah in reprimanding God's people of this grievous act that pains the heart of Father God (Matt. 15:8).

Calling the Father *"Abba"* or even *"Papa"* does not minimize holy reverence for Him. It simply expresses who He is to us in a deep understanding of our cherished identity in Him. Calling God *"Abba"* is one of the highest ways of revering Him, because it conveys an attitude, not of presumptuous familiarity, but as a beloved child close to Father's heart. It is an honoring expression of a dependent child. After all, this is how we are to enter our Father's Kingdom, as a child. And yet, as I said, it is more than that; it speaks of our identity as mature sons and daughters.

Living in the reality of God as our Abba Father is what Jesus teaches us. We must be a people who know how to tremble in God's presence, and yet know His intimate fathering care. Too often, religion has taught us to be *reverent* but not *intimate* with God. God wants to deliver us from every empty, dead religious structure that prevents us from experiencing His presence. God wants to immerse us in Himself so that we are not only spiritually reborn, but also nurtured for a life of authority in the Son.

Jesus came with a new paradigm in which we *revere* God as we learn to love Him with all of our heart, as a true son or daughter. Such a life respects what He says, *and* yet climbs into the warmth of His embrace and says, *"My Father, Dad."*

Jesus said that to enter the Kingdom of heaven we must be changed and be as little children (Matt. 18:3). The nature of a child is that they are simple, and they believe what you tell them. They are trusting, forgiving, and are completely dependent. But foremost, a child looks to the parent as their source of help, guidance, protection, and provision. A child depends on a parent for everything.

Abba wants us to relate to Him—not in distant living—but as holy children in relationship with a **Holy Father**. He wants us to believe Him, look to Him, and trust Him as He lifts us up into divine purpose. He delights in us—in you and me—and He wants us to know a rich delight in Him. He also intends that we revere Him as greater than ourselves. After all, He is.

LIFE IN THE SON

Though sin separated man from God's presence, the sacrifice of Jesus brings us back to the Father's house and His embrace. Here we learn to be *Father-centered*, rather than being *self-centered*. This is something that every child of God must learn.

Abba sent Jesus not merely as "a" way, but as the only way to Himself. No other person, religion, or ideology has ever—nor can ever—open the realm of God's fathering presence to us but Jesus.

He is the Door to Father's house and the Way to Abba's arms where we are restored to **identity and purpose**...two dynamics searched for and longed for by every human heart.

King Solomon, one of the greatest kings on earth, said he had looked everywhere in the world to find what *satisfies*. He experienced it all, but only found emptiness (Ecclesiastes). The ultimate satisfying of a human life, especially in the areas of identity and purpose, can only be found in intimacy with the One who created us for a divine purpose, and who loves us.

The immensity of Abba Father's love for us is seen in *His* own sacrifice in sending Jesus to the cross. We typically see the Son's sacrificial part, but only from our point of view as a redeemed life. But Abba Father also experienced a tremendous sacrifice. In my own role as a parent, I have learned that a father or mother would rather give their own life than to see harm come to their child.

When Jesus declared that He and the Father are one, it meant that Abba Father was just as much involved in the crucifixion as Jesus was (John 10:30). Father sent Him. He was there. He saw. He felt. He agonized, as well as rejoiced...He was *in* the Son working out our salvation.

Our restoration back to God came at a great cost as Father "sowed" His Son into the earth, like a "seed," to bring forth a powerful harvest of sons and daughters in His likeness—sons and daughters of glory. From Jesus death, burial and resurrection has come millions of "branches" from the Vine who are now filling the earth and releasing the fruit of the Father's Kingdom.

Our Heavenly Brother's willingness paid the penalty for our sin, breaking the yoke of a counterfeit framework. He took the curse that was on us and makes us a new creation—a son or daughter who know the Heavenly Father as *Abba Father*.

I love how the Godhead work together for our maturing as sons and daughters. The Father sends the Holy Spirit to reveal truth to our heart regarding sin and our need for Christ; we come to Jesus (whom the Father also sent) and He brings us back into fellowship with the Father; the Father and Son send the Spirit to endue us with power from above for the work we are to do as Abba's sons and daughters.

Even as I write this, I realize that human words cannot truly express the amazing divine mystery that takes place in us when we are born again of God's Spirit. It is a marvelous miracle and mystery of how the Father, Son, and Holy Spirit work intimately together and with us. If we don't have the Son, we don't have life, because without Christ we have neither the Father or the Spirit (1 John 5:11-12).

THE SPIRIT OF ADOPTION

The Holy Spirit is called the *Spirit of Adoption*. He brings us into the position of being a legal heir of God with all accompanying rights and privileges. As sons and daughters of God, we are co-heirs together with the Father's Firstborn, Jesus. We are positioned to legally inherit our Father's Kingdom with Him (Gal. 4:7). [3]

We are no longer slaves to sin or orphans left alone in this world. We are no longer fatherless (John 14:18). We do not have to "figure things out" for ourselves. We belong to the Heavenly Family. We have continual access to Father's counsel and to all His resources.

The Spirit of Adoption gives us a new framework for a new way of thinking and living—no longer for ourselves, but for *Abba Father.*

Being parented by God creates a new mindset for how we perceive and engage life on earth. Here are a few differences in a mindset of being "fathered" by God versus how we lived with an "orphan" or "fatherless" mindset.

A "Fathered" Mindset	vs.	A "Fatherless" Mindset
Sense of belonging		Sense of abandonment
Grounded in love		Spirit of rejection
Identity as Abba's child		Identity in things, others

"Fathered" vs. "Fatherless" Mindset continued...

Sees God as loving	Sees God as a taskmaster
Has hope in God	Hopes in circumstances
Engages works of faith	Strives, Legalistic
Rests in God's affirmation	Seeks approval of others
Enjoys fellowship with God	Feels God is distant
Looks to God for all things	Tries to fill own needs
Trusts in God	Is suspicious
Has peace	Worries, is anxious
Is led by grace	Is performance driven
Feels radiant within	Feels shame, condemnation
Is confident in God	Is insecure
Receives God's counsel	Is self-guided
Honors, prefers others	Is jealous of others
Forgives	Accuses, blames others
Seeks the good of others	Has selfish ambition
Seeks inter-connection, unity	Seeks own path
Seeks comfort in God	Comfort in others, things
Celebrates who they are	Compares self with others
Lives in freedom	Lives in bondage

Our mindsets govern our choices in life. They govern our behavior and our path of destiny, for good or bad. The *Holy Spirit of Adoption* frees us from living as one who is abandoned, lost, or alone. He grounds us in the Father's love, and fills the deepest places of our heart with God's love (Rom. 5:5). We are no longer slaves to fear or bondage.

In Hebrew culture of the Old Testament, adopted sons had the same rights, privileges, and standing as a birth-son. They were embraced no differently than a natural born son, and took on the father's name. In fact, parents were held more accountable for an adopted child as special laws were designed and enacted to protect them from abuse or abandonment.

Everything that the Father gave to Jesus, the Holy Spirit shares with us, including the responsibilities and affairs of Father's Kingdom (James 2:5). We are heirs of the same Kingdom of power that Jesus demonstrated and proclaimed saying, *"Repent, for the kingdom of heaven is at hand"* (Matt. 4:17). In Christ, we not only receive a new life with intentional purpose and power to live it out, but a new culture, government, and work on earth.

Our Heavenly Father has given us everything we need to live as His sons and daughters. It's time to break free of every ideology that keeps us in distant living as religious servants rather than anointed sons and daughters. It's time to step into the bond of family love and know Him as our Abba, our Papa. In so doing, we honor Him by drawing near to Him, taking on His name, and opening our heart to meet with His.

Father, thank You that we can know You as Papa.

PERSONAL APPLICATION:

1. How do you see Abba Father in relationship with you? Involved? Distant?

2. In what ways do you depend on the Holy Spirit in your life?

3. What are the different revelations God has given you of Himself?

4. Do you feel like you have a "fathered" mindset or a "fatherless" mindset?

5. How does it make you feel to call God *"Dad"* or *"Papa"*?

CHAPTER 6

WHO IS YOUR FATHER?

"My father was my teacher, but most importantly he was a great dad." — *Beau Bridges* [1]

Some people never get to know their earthly fathers. Some people know them well, while others know them a little. Some fathers don't know how to be relational, but Abba Father is *very* relational and wants us to know Him. He is a wonderful Father.

How do I know this to be true? By experience, by His Word, and by the testimony of others and history itself. Just look at how wonderfully He has brought His Holy Word into our hands that we might know Him. God's Spirit intentionally moved on the hearts of more than forty men, over a period of 1600 years, to write, under His inspiration, the sixty-six books we know as the Holy Bible, the *Word of God*. These writers were fishermen, farmers, kings, prophets, judges, doctors, and shepherds—men of diverse backgrounds, yet inspired by One—God.

God's Spirit spoke to these men and had them write His words so that we can know God *and* who we are to Him, and in Him, and that we might understand His love for mankind. The Holy Bible is Abba Father's love letter to humanity. It is a privilege to have the Father's words.

Life with Abba Father

There is a yearning in the heart of every human being to know their parents. It is why adopted children often seek to know their biological parents when possible. It's why we do ancestry researches. People want to know what their parents were like. Were they good people? Where did they live? What were their experiences? What did they do? What did they believe? What did they look like...do we look like them?

In reality, these questions are simply part of a bigger picture that we want the answers to: Who am I? Why do I exist? Why am I here? The Heavenly Father delights to answer these bigger picture questions for us through relationship with Him. He desires that we know Him as more than just words on a page or a distant Creator. He fashioned the key of intimacy with Him as the doorway to knowing our own identity. The more we know the Holy Trinity personally, the more we know exactly who we are, why we exist, and why we are here. We also know what we are to do.

Jesus, as Abba's Firstborn, modeled this very truth to us; He knew exactly who He was and why He was here. He knew Father intimately and kept in complete unity with Holy Spirit. He lived out His life and purpose in the embrace of being Abba's Son.

The very fact that God bestows on us the incredible title of being "His children" demonstrates His heart toward us (1 John 3:1-3). He could have called us: subjects, slaves, servants, maids, purchased objects, owned items, etc., but He didn't. He calls us His sons and daughters, and He wants to raise us as such.

Let's look at what Scripture says about God as a *Father*.

1   THE FATHER OF ALL LIFE

The nature of our Father is to create and bring forth life. He is the Creator and source of life, making Him *creation's Father* (Gen. 1; Acts 17:25). He is the Author of created things—both living and non-living, seen and unseen. He arranged worlds (the universe and perpetuity of times) by His spoken word and brought into existence what is seen from what is not seen (Heb. 11:3).

90

God created the heavens and stretched them out, He formed the earth and what springs from it, and He gives breath and spirit to the people who walk in it (Isa. 42:5). When we look at creation, we see the expression of the Father of creation. We see His creative design, power, order, authority, beauty, and His mysteries. We can know about Him through every aspect of what He has done and brought forth. The very existence of creation around us, and in us, holds us responsible and without excuse regarding the knowledge that we, indeed, have a Creator (Rom. 1:20).

As the Father of life, He is above all and in everything (Eph. 4:6). Without Him nothing exists. **Creation is purposeful, intentional, has *one* Father, and we exist *for* Him** (1 Cor. 8:6). He is Eternal and never sleeps, but watches over His creation continually, ever working to prosper His beautiful plan with what He has brought forth into existence (Ps. 121:3).

At creation, Father called out our destiny before we even appeared—He calls things that don't yet exist as though they already do (Rom. 4:17). When it was time for us to appear, He formed us in our mother's womb, having already written in His book the very details of who we are and the days we will walk here on earth (Ps. 139). He is our Father and we are the purposeful and delightful work of *His* hands (Isa. 64:8; Rev. 4:11).

As human beings made in His likeness, we are the creation of His desire. In Him our existence has life, movement, and purpose (Gen. 1: 27; Acts 17:28).

Father not only creates life, but He is able to resurrect back to life what has lost living energy—physically and spiritually. The Son also carries His Father's same power (Gal. 1:1; Rom. 6:4; Jn. 5:21).

As God's creation, we cannot create something from nothing or resurrect a dead spirit to life, but in Christ we have the power of the Holy Spirit to heal the sick and raise the dead back to life. We can inspire spiritual life in others by speaking the living words of God, and being the tangible touch of His love that gives life-giving encouragement, hope, and faith in Him (Matt. 10:8).

2   ABBA IS A GARDENER

As the Author of life, our Father is also a *Husbandman*—a skilled Gardener and Caretaker of the life He brings into existence. He is committed to the full growth and prosperity of His creation, to us. Jesus Himself referred to Abba Father as the *Heavenly Vinedresser* and Himself as the *True Vine*. It was an expression of how He saw Abba Father as being intricately involved in overseeing His life and growth. The first Adam had proved to be *untrue* (unfaithful) through rebellion to Father's command, but Jesus faithfully obeyed His Father. As He did, it empowered Jesus to fulfill His mission on earth.

Isaiah prophesied that the Messiah (Jesus) would be the Father's **"tender plant"** (Isa. 53:2). The Hebrew word for *"tender plant"* (*"yowneq"²*) means: suckling, sapling, young plant. It is one that receives life and nutrients from another plant, as a baby from a mother. Jesus lived and matured as Son of Man through absolute dependence of Father's words and the presence of His Spirit.

When Jesus said, "Man shall not live by bread alone, but by every Word that proceeds from the mouth of God," He wasn't rehearsing a good ideology, it was Jesus' reality (Matt. 4:4). He knew that He would never fulfill His intended life purpose on earth apart from the unhindered hearing of His Father's words, counsel, and direction. He, the Vine, continually looked to Abba, by the Holy Spirit, as His Vinedresser.

A *husbandman*, by definition, is a *worker of the ground*. God loves to work with ground. Look at what incredible things He brought forth at creation from the ground—He formed from the ground a man in His own likeness—Adam. And *from* the man, He formed a bride also in His own likeness. God called them Adam, blessed them, and commanded them to be fruitful, multiply and rule the earth together.

As God's children, they were also husbandmen—caretakers of the earth realm. This caretaking assignment was natural *and* spiritual in nature for which they had full access to divine provision.

This commission to guard and prosper the earth has never ceased. As Abba's children, we carry our Father's likeness as the earth's husbandmen, protecting it and prospering it the way Father designs it to be—with full life. God gives each of us spheres of influence and territory where we are to be guardians, using our gifts and abilities to prosper the land and its inhabitants.

A garden is *a specific area of ground* dedicated to a specific growth of life. In Scripture, *ground* can represent either natural land or the soil of our heart—both are places designed to receive seed and nurture its growth, whatever that seed may be (we will talk more about the soil of our heart in a moment).

The work of a husbandman is to make sure the soil is kept fertile and life in the garden prospering and protected from predators that try to steal seed and devour its growth and fruitfulness. Neglect to protect and prosper right seed makes the garden vulnerable to destruction, and thus, the failure of an intended harvest is experienced.

Our Father is a husbandman and He is laboring for an intended harvest with mankind. He is raising us to be His heirs.

A garden, as a place where seed grows, is important to God. In Scripture, we see a number of significant eternal activities that took place in gardens—just look at the following:

➢ Man's commission from God began in a garden (Gen. 2:8).

➢ Man's bride was drawn from his side in a garden (Gen. 2:21-24).

➢ Satan visited mankind in a garden to sow mistrust, unbelief and rebellion in his heart toward God (Gen. 3).

➢ God referred to Himself as a *husbandman* and Israel as His *vineyard* (Isa. 5).

➢ In the Song of Solomon, the beloved of the king is described as a garden (Song of Sol. 4:15).

➢ Jesus embraced the *cup of suffering* in a garden (Mark 14:32-41).

> ➢ Jesus was buried and raised to life in a garden (John 19:38-42).
> ➢ Our heart is like a garden where God's Word is sown (Mark 4:1-20).

ABBA'S GARDENING IN OUR LIFE

Our life is like a garden. While Father is our Head Caretaker, we also co-labor with Him, the Son and the Holy Spirit for a beautiful harvest in our life—one that glorifies God in the earth. Our care is never outside our Father's watchful eye as He works on our behalf with understanding and skill (Isa. 40:28)...even if we don't always see Him at work. He is there. He is near. He is caring. He is working to prosper our life with eternal purposes in view.

Like Abba's Firstborn, we are also Father's "tender plants." We are completely dependent on Him. Listening to His voice is key to our full growth and maturity as His child. Father speaks to us through His written Word and to our spirit-man by His Spirit, speaking in myriad ways to reveal to us His heart, mind, counsel, and love. As gardeners with Him, we are to be watchful in cultivating our heart and life as a place where His words have a favorable place to grow.

Abba Father is *committed* to us and our fruitfulness as His children. He does not abandon us, forget us, or neglect us. He loves us perfectly. He works to develop our life with vision of a specific harvest regarding who we are and our assignment as His son or daughter. He is committed to the seed of His Word that He speaks to us—a word that He says, "...will not return to Me void, but it shall accomplish that which I please, and it shall prosper in the thing whereto I sent it" (Isa. 55:11). He watches over His Word to bring it to full fruition (Jer. 1:12).

As a wise Gardener, Father knows what to do in each season of our life. Just as He placed the celestial bodies of light to govern earth's natural seasons, so He governs our spiritual seasons and times with divine government and illumination. I personally can see different seasons in my life. In some I have experienced the refreshing wind of breakthrough in circumstances. In other seasons my soul has felt the dryness as of a hard winter. And yet, there He is at work in both.

Like a good gardener, Father weeds out what doesn't belong in *His* garden. If He didn't plant it, then it probably doesn't have a *good* reason for being there (Jer. 31:28; Matt. 15:13). Weeds are undesirable plants that can spring up in our life, growing from seed that doesn't come from God. The storms of life or troubling circumstances easily drop seeds of doubt and fear into our heart. Birds, which may represent demonic activity as negative thoughts or temptation, can also drop seed in our soil. It's important to identify *what* is growing in our garden.

Other types of weeds have root systems that crawl into places where they don't belong. Ungodly mindsets in culture can easily crawl into our thinking to establish themselves in our belief systems. Colossians 2:8 says to **beware** **of worldly philosophies, empty deception, and man's traditions that are not of Christ.** These mindsets subtly crawl into our thinking from worldly influences and false religious doctrines, taking our mind captive to wrong belief systems.

While Satan wars against our minds, it is the condition of our heart that determines whether his seeds take root in us or not. God's Word instructs us to guard our heart because out of it spring the issues of life, and because the heart is easily deceived (Prov. 4:23; Jer. 17:9). In fact, scientific study has discovered that the heart actually has a "brain" that monitors the validity and integrity of our thoughts.

Thoughts are determined as "right" or "wrong" and then kept or thrown out according to the condition of our heart. It is with the heart that we make our choices in life and keep or toss the seeds that fall on our soil.

Father's work in our garden is constant. There are times He will "prune us" and have us rest from some of our labor, preparing us for new fruitfulness. At other times He will work deep to prepare our heart for new revelation. He works to break down hard places and remove stones of unbelief. He is ever working to make our heart a rich place for His Voice to flourish in us.

God's processes in the garden of our heart and life can at times be painful to our flesh, but the result will be increase in spiritual life. While our Father comforts us, He doesn't coddle us—He is, after all, raising sons and daughters for ruling the earth and reconciling nations to His designs through His counsel and governmental authority. And that, is no small task.

Some people ask, "If God watches over all things, then why does He allow so much suffering and pain in the world?" I don't know the full answer to this, but I do know that God did not initiate the pain we experience in this world; the first Adam opened that door of darkness through agreement with Satan who is the father of lies and destruction. Satan is a liar who steals and destroys life, and it is mankind's agreement with his words that continues to promote destruction in our lives, relationships, and in this world.

We do have a way, however, to stop the pain. We do this by following Jesus and allowing Abba to parent us. As we set our eyes on Christ, we learn to walk as Abba's care-takers of the earth with spiritual authority to destroy the works of darkness—in our own soul and in this world over which Father sets us as kings and priests. We labor with Jesus to restore the wellbeing of our life, family and communities. The earth itself is waiting and longing for us to do this (Rom. 8:19).

3 THE FATHER OF GLORY

Ephesians 1:17 calls God the *Father of glory*. The word "glory" in referring to God is difficult to define with mere human words. It's like trying to explain the brilliance of God Himself. Glory has to do with the fullness of God and the infinite radiance of who He is.

In Exodus 34:6-7, God described His glory as the divine substance of His love, compassion, patience, mercy, kindness, truth, and forgiveness...all rolled into one. Israel, having been freed from captivity described it as God's greatness, His voice, His fire, and His presence (Deut. 5:24).

God's glory is supernatural, transformational power. It so transformed the appearance of Moses that people couldn't look on his face as it shone with *glory radiance* (Exod. 34:30, 33). God's glory is His power that opens the way for our crossing into His full purposes—as when Israel carried the ark of God's glory when crossing the Jordan River (Josh. 4:7). His glory is incomparable power that defeats the enemy (1 Sam. 5).

I love God's glory because it was His glory that transformed my life. It manifested in the kindness of His voice toward me, His gracious Spirit that taught me, and His love that drew my heart toward Him. It manifested through the people He sent into my life to help me. It was displayed in the wisdom He brought me through mentors who showed me how to defeat the enemy that wanted to destroy my life. It radiated in the tangible awareness of His presence strengthening me and letting me know He cared.

In John 17:5, Jesus described the Father's glory as intimacy and oneness with Him. The whole mission of the cross was to lead countless *sons and daughters* out of death and into glory. The apostle Paul described God's glory as the fountain of wisdom and revelation that opens the eyes of our understanding to know God, to know His call on our life, and *His* inheritance in *us*. God's glory unveils the greatness of His power toward us (Eph. 1:17-19).

It was the Father's glory, the manifest fullness of Himself, that raised Jesus from the dead; it is that same glory that raises us out of a dead state into a new life in Christ (Rom. 6:4). The power of resurrection life comes from God's glory.

We were made to know the realm of glory. Jesus warned us not to seek the glory that comes from people (an earthly glory), but the glory that comes from our Father (John 5:44; Rom. 2:7; John 8:50). Jesus came to earth wrapped in the humble garment of a little human baby, but His second coming will be in the majestic display of His Father's *glory*, accompanied by an angelic host (Mark 8:38).

97

The Father does not share His glory with idols or false gods, but He does share it with His Son who is the *exact* expression of His likeness (Isa. 42:8; 48:10, 11).

The Father works to free our heart from idols so that we too can participate with Him in His glory. Moses said, "Lord, let me know You; show me Your glory." God created us to be carriers of His radiance—temples of His light and glory. It's what sets us apart as His sons and daughters—His family.

4   THE FATHER OF LIGHTS

The Apostle James called God the Father of lights from whom every good and perfect gift comes down to us, and that with Him is never any change, fluctuation, or dimming in His brilliance—there is no darkness in Him, at all, ever. There is no dark hidden agenda (James 1:17). He is the Father of lights because He Himself IS light (1 John 1:5).

The word *"light"* (Grk: *"phos"*) means: to bring or give light as seen by the eye, and, metaphorically, as reaching the mind. It refers to anything that emits illumination: stars, fire, as well as the enlightenment of truth, understanding, wisdom, and even favor. **Light is linked with authority over darkness**.

God created each star in the heavens, and each has its own place and brilliancy. He flung them purposefully into constellations with the divine assignment to not only govern the days and seasons of earth, but their very alignment in the heavens tell the story of redemption. Psalm 19:1-2 says that the heavens *speak* day to day and night to night, displaying the knowledge of God.

Astrology has twisted the meaning of God's design in the stars and made a false worship of them. But the truth, is they speak of Jesus! The Gospel of creation and redemption is pictorially displayed in the patterns that stars create. Each constellation declares God's glorious plan with mankind. No one could have done that but God! For example, the constellation Aires speaks of the sacrificial ram or Lamb slain for us; Lyra, the harp, speaks of praise;

98

Coma (the woman and Child), speaks of the child who is the *Desire of the Nations*; Crux reveals the Cross; Andromeda (the chained woman) speaks of the captive daughter of Zion to be set free; and Leo declares the Lion of Judah.[3]

I could go on, but as you can see, God set the stars in place to declare His glory and the wonder of His work with mankind.

Another beautiful dynamic of these heavenly fires that burn in the darkness is that they sing. Stellar seismology can actually record the sounds of the stars, sounds that indicate what is going on inside the star's interior. In the ancient book of Job, he understood the sound of these luminary fires in the heavens to be worship — the song of creation praising the Father together with the angels for His goodness (Job 38:7).

Jesus, the Bright and Morning Star and Light of the world, said that in Him, we too are the light of the world (Rev. 22:16; Matt. 5:14-16). The fire of the Holy Spirit and light of truth in our inner man is what makes us burning luminaries in this dark world, shining the way for others to also know the path of life.

THE NATURE OF LIGHT IS GOVERNMENTAL

The light of God is given us to shine with His dominion and ruling power over darkness. Light is the divine energy, power, and ability to understand divine mysteries, and by which we move in unity with God. And just as with the stars, Abba Father sets us into specific places, locales, and relationships. He appoints our place where He wants us to be and to declare the work of His hands.

This is why it is important to know the gifts and specific call He places on our life, and give intentionality to preparing ourselves regarding those gifts. If He has appointed us to be a pastor and we are sitting in a business office somewhere, we will not shine in the scope and capacity designed for us by our Father. This is just as true if we want to be a pastor, but He has called us to business. We must seek to know what He has called us to do for our assignment on earth.

As we are in our appointed place, Father will also connect us with divine relationships that, together, creates a synergy (multiplied radiance in gifts and anointing) for revealing Christ to our communities. As we shine together, the unity releases multiplied increase of the knowledge of Christ. My gift alone has a specific sphere of influence, but combined with others and their gifts, the scope of influence increases. Multiplication is an aspect of both divine blessings and command.

As Abba's children, our life is about His glory being revealed in the earth. In this hour, there is a fresh call of God for unity of the Christ's body—each member functioning in their place, and with others, to declare His story and release His government.

Even in our dark times, God's light over us never dims. Micah 7:8 says, "When I sit in darkness, the Lord will be a light to me." Darkness does not have the "final say!" God's goodness toward us never ceases, and what He gives us is perfect and complete. When our heart is shadowed by the enemy's taunting, we may view what we have as insufficient or *not* good, but gratitude removes the veil of doubt and mistrust so that our eyes see God's goodness that follows us all our days (1 Thess. 5:18; Ps. 23:6).

As we walk in the midst of this world, in good times and bad, Father designed the divine light within us to releases its song as worship to Him. As His "stars," we govern the earth from heavenly places, releasing the sound of praise as we declare the story of redemption.

5 A MERCIFUL FATHER

Abba Father is the source of mercy. He is the *Father of Mercies* and *God of all Comfort*. The word *mercies* (Grk. *"oiktirmos"*) means: heart of compassion for the ills of others. It is the nature of being compassionate, affectionate, loving, and tender toward the weak, and is part of His manifest glory (2 Cor. 1:3; Exod. 34:6). As children, we need the abundance of His compassions and comforts in so many areas. His mercies are new every morning and they remind

Him continually of His covenants, including His covenant with us (Ps. 106:45; Lam. 3:22, 23).

Father's compassion and mercies cover *all* His works (Ps. 145:9). Think about that for a moment—everything that He brings into existence is blanketed and kept under the protection and provision of His never ending affection and tenderness. His great mercy is the foundation by which we are called His children, empowering us to live with *continual* hope and unceasing expectation in Him (1 Pet. 1:3).

Our Father is *merciful* and gentle toward us because He knows our weakness and fragile make-up. He is mindful that we are made from mere dust (Ps. 103:13-14). He is patient when we falter and stumble, not condemning us, but helping us. He is compassionate with the sick; gentle with the ignorant; and merciful with the repentant child.

Abba delights in our victories, and grieves at our waywardness. But no matter where we are at in life, in His great love for us, He sees us as *"containers of mercy"* designed to receive the abundance of His provision (Rom. 9:23). Father's mercy toward us is rich with healing and deliverance, resting on those who revere Him, so that His glory dwells in their land (Ps. 103:17; Ps. 85:9).

As Abba Father's children, Jesus said that we, too, are to be merciful like our Father (Luke 6:36). We are to *love* mercy—it is one of Father's "lifestyle requirements" for *all* mankind (Mic. 6:8). God, who hears the cries of the hurting and needy continually, says we are to hear their cries, too . . . and take action! We are His hands of mercy in the earth, and as we show mercy to others, we, too, will receive mercy (Matt. 5:7).

6 A FATHER TO THE FATHERLESS
AND JUDGE OF WIDOWS

Our Father's nature is justice—impartial fairness in doing what is right. His face looks toward the poor, the fatherless, and the widow, and He is deeply moved by the helpless and commands us to provide for those in need. This is so important to Him that He says if we deliberately ignore the needs of the poor, our own cry will not be heard, and we will reap curses (Prov. 28:27; 21:13).

Abba Father cares for those who have no fathers, and promises that when our earthly parents fail or forsake us, He will gather us into His own arms (Ps. 27:10). And because His eyes are on us and promises to care for us, He is adamant about our care for the fatherless. We are to be the tangible hands of His care for them—it is the heart of *true* **religion** (Ps. 68:5; James 1:27).

Our Father is also a judge, a righteous advocate and defender, to another group that His eyes are attentive to—the widows. In general, a widow can be vulnerable because of the loss of a spouse, and may be in need financially, or without needed help and proper support. We hear reports all the time about those who prey on the elderly, and especially on elderly women, seeking to take advantage of their vulnerability. As a righteous judge, He works on their behalf and commands us to protect them, provide for them, help them, and be just in our dealings with them.

7 FATHER IS A MAN OF WAR

While our Father is kind toward us as a judge and defender of the weak, **He is also a Man of War—a Champion of Battle** (Exod. 15:3). And He never loses. He is not only compassionate, but He is also powerful, and moves mightily for what is good and right, and for what belongs to Him.

His arms are not just comforting, they are mighty in war, and His resources and strategies for our victory in every area of life are limitless and available. He is, after all, the Champion of battle—no matter how big our giants in life look like, He is greater. This is our Dad.

King David, in the Old Testament, understood God's warrior nature in conjunction with His justice. He doesn't simply go forth to conquer, but to set things right, to bring about justice and righteous judgments and ruling in the earth where chaos and lawlessness have prevailed. These also are part of His nature. King David understood that God appoints rulers to both care for the people *and* defend them from enemies. Even before David became king, he slew giants who harassed God's people with the intent of taking their divine inheritance away from them. And before that, as a young shepherd, he tenderly led his father's flock *and* killed lions and bears seeking to hurt the flock.

I'm grateful for how my Father cares for me *and* went to war on my behalf through Christ. He didn't leave me in my condition, but worked to free me from the power of sin and death that had a strong hold on my life. Jesus, Son of David, joined with Abba Father in His vengeance and judgment against sin on the cross (Luke 16:19-31, Luke 13:3, John 15:1-11).

As Abba's children, we are also called to war on the behalf of others—to free them from the death-grip of darkness that holds them captive.

Our Father is a good and mighty Father who keenly watches over the earth, and over us. We have read in this chapter of who He is as the source of life, glory, lights, and mercy, as well as a Father to orphans and defender of widows, and a Man of War. These are just a few aspects of how He reveals Himself through His Word and in our life. The more we learn who He is, the more we see there is to know of Him. The knowledge of God is ever unfolding!

Father, thank You for the amazing wonders of who You are!

PERSONAL APPLICATION:

1. In what ways do you see Father caring for your life?

2. In what ways does Father want you to guard your heart? What seeds are growing in it?

3. How does Father want you to protect the world around

you? How does He want you to prosper it and "work the land"?

4. In what ways have you seen or experienced God's glory?

5. Do you know your gifts and appointed place?

6. Who are your right alignments?

7. In what ways have you experienced Father's mercies?

8. How are you merciful to others?

9. In what ways do you help the poor, fatherless, and widows?

10. In what ways are you engaging with Father in the warfare of setting others free?

CHAPTER 7

THE FATHER *and* HIS SONS

*"It is not flesh and blood, but the heart which
makes us fathers and sons."*
—*Johann Friedrich Von Schiller* [1]

In this chapter, we are going to continue looking at who Abba Father is, but more specifically with *whom* He interacts as a near Father, and how His sons and daughters interact with Him. Let's see what God's Word reveals about these beautiful relationships.

1 ABBA FATHER AND JESUS

*"So that with one accord you may with one voice glorify the God and
Father of our Lord Jesus Christ." (Rom. 15:6)*

The more we see how Jesus was parented by Abba Father, the greater understanding we have of Abba's fathering in our own life and being a part of His family. Jesus lived from the framework of an identity anchored in intimate relationship with Abba. He viewed His life as having full provision from Abba for all His needs. He carried the same core values as His Father, values such as love, mercy and truth. He put His expectations in His Father and not in people, though He loved people. His life-focus was His Father, doing His Father's work, and delighting His Father's heart.

Delighting God's heart is what we were created for—to bring Him *"pleasure"* (Rev. 4:11). We not only exist *by* God, but also *for* Him (2 Cor. 6:18; 1 Cor. 8:6). The Greek word for *"pleasure"* (*"thelema"*) means: what one wishes, purposes, or desires. Mankind wasn't created to live separate from God, but to be His family carrying out divine intentions on earth. As Son of Man, Jesus understood this and lived it. His entire work was to restore mankind to this place of bringing God pleasure.

EYES AND EARS TOWARD THE FATHER

As we saw earlier, eating from the tree of the knowledge of good and evil in the Garden of Eden, shifted mankind's perspectives, framework, and patterns of response. Because Jesus' framework was family life with the Father and Holy Spirit, His "inner radar" was always searching for the mind and perceptions of His Father. He didn't lean on His own understanding, but looked to the Father's understanding and counsel (Prov. 3:5).

Scientific studies actually show that every one of us has an "internal radar"—an inner "scanner" that looks for patterns of connection by which we live and make decisions. Our radar determines what we adopt *and* reject as being truth, or not. Science calls it *"patternicity."*

Dr. Scott Huettel, professor of psychology and behavioral science, teaches how the human brain looks for structures and patterns in the world. He says, "We are set up to find patterns...to extract regularity from the world."[2] In other words, the brain looks for patterns in an effort to make sense of complicated information. This ability of the brain to find patterns enables us to function in a complex world. However, the brain may also establish wrong conclusions by supplying assumed information that is not actually there, or overlooking information it thinks does not fit the pattern or is part of the situation. [3]

How does this relate to Jesus, us, and Abba Father? In every way! Jesus looked to the Father for His pattern of thinking *and* conclusions regarding every circumstance of life on earth. His "radar" looked to Abba's thoughts for answers and solutions. The Father gave the Son the *right* views, including where He came from, where He was going, and what He was to do. Thus He declared that Father was **greater than Himself** and honored Him as such (John 14:28; 16:28).

It is this connection with the Father that we are brought into through the Son. Scripture says we are to fix our eyes on the Son, the One whose gaze is fixed on the Father (Heb. 12:2). This gaze did not make Jesus a robot who couldn't think for Himself. No! What it made Him was the Ruler He was born to be. The Father taught Him to discern right from wrong, good from evil, and what is holy versus what is unholy. And so He grew *strong in spirit* with *wisdom and grace* as Abba's Son (Luke 2:40). He increased in obedience to His Father through life experiences (Heb. 5:8). He practiced walking out His human journey with divine counsel.

On earth, Jesus didn't experience perfect circumstances. He too had an earthly family: a human step-dad (Joseph), a human mother (Mary), four younger very human brothers and a few sisters. He lived with imperfect human parents and religious siblings who didn't believe in Him (until He left earth), and, no doubt, He was taunted about His mother's pregnancy while carrying Him as not being the "righteous norm." The townspeople viewed Him merely as "the carpenter's son," and religious leaders viewed His hometown as "what good can come from Nazareth?" What more do I need to say?

Painful interactions could have established wrong patterns in Jesus' mind about Himself, but Jesus' heart was connected to His Heavenly Father. He didn't negate His human emotions, but felt them, acknowledged them, and processed them in a healthy way—with His Father. He experienced losses and disappointments, but He also placed His trust in His Father. Jesus' "radar" looked for His Father's pattern of thinking and way of doing things. As Jesus Himself said, "The ruler of the world [Satan] is coming, and he has nothing in Me" (John 14:30). In other words, there was no agreement in Jesus' heart or mind with fear and hopeless perspectives. He was anchored in His Father's nearness and strength.

THINKING THE FATHER'S THOUGHTS

As Abba's Son, Jesus did not embrace the *ways* of the spirit of this world to guide Him. He did, however, discern their presence, judged the spirits driving them, and dealt with them through His Father's authority and with righteous judgment.

Psalm 78 speaks about God's sons who did not set their heart right toward Him, and thus their thinking wasn't right. This caused them to draw back from moving with God to war for their inheritance from Him. Scriptures reveals that the heart and mind are linked, for thoughts spring from the *heart* (Mark 7:21). Having a right "radar" includes a heart that knows God, discerns the enemy, *and* brings our thoughts captive into obedience to the mind of Christ. Scripture says that, "The weapons of our warfare are not of the flesh, but divinely powerful for the destruction of fortresses. *We are* destroying speculations and every lofty thing raised up against the knowledge of God, and *we are* taking every thought captive to the obedience of the Son (2 Cor. 10:4-5).

Thinking the Father's thoughts includes discerning our thoughts (think about what we are thinking about) and aligning our mind with God's Word. This empowers us to recognize Satan's lies, deceptions, and accusations, and deal with them through the truth of God and power of His Spirit. Jesus didn't let people's opinions paralyze Him, circumstances derail Him, or anxiety shape His moods, choices, or responses. He discerned error, bad counsel, and false judgments and righteously dealt with them (see Ps. 1).

We have been given this same mind that Christ had (1 Cor. 2:16). As sons, we have a new pattern of thinking, seeing, perceiving, and knowing, and thus, a new way of experiencing life with the Father. Having God's thoughts is having His heart.

The Son came as the Word—the voice—of the Father. Jesus said that mankind doesn't live by mere physical food, but what proceeds from God speaking to us (Matt. 4:4). In the Garden of Eden, God's children listened to another voice. In fact, one of the questions God asked the man was, "Who told you that…?"

The Greek term *"word,"* here in Matthew 4, is *"rhema"* and means: the *living speech* of God. In essence, Jesus came to earth as the living, breathing speech of the Father. Our body may be empowered by healthy food (which came by God speaking—Gen. 1), but our entire life, purpose, and destiny is empowered by the speaking of God. This is why Abba sent His WORD to rescue us and translate us from death to life. Jesus, the *Living* Word, not only gives us Father's thoughts, but He also gives us the Holy Spirit to give us understanding as we read God's *written* Word.

As I shared earlier, I know what it is to have the lies of the enemy find a place of habitation in my thinking. I agreed with wrong thoughts and made wrong choices. I know what it is to draw conclusions from skewed frameworks and a "radar" that looked to myself for answers. I also know now what it is to have the mind of Christ and it is a beautiful thing!

Having a mind that searches and finds its answers and solutions in the realms of light means hope, positive expectations, freedom from the tyranny of the flesh and from the lies of demonic oppression. It's a mind that knows its identity in the Father. It experiences the real presence of Abba's love and Holy Spirit's comfort and tutorage in truth. It is a mind that knows both rest and courage in a family framework with the Father, Son, and Holy Spirit.

REVEALING THE FATHER'S HEART

Abba Father *delights* to fill the Son with His own *fullness*—giving Jesus ALL that HE has. So too it delights Abba Father to give us HIS fullness in His Son (Col. 1:19, 20; John 1:16). This full provision of God empowered the Son for His life and work, which was, according to Jesus, the Father working through Him. That's why Jesus said, "If you've seen Me, you've seen the Father" (John

14:9-10; 12:49, 50; 8:26, 28). **The Son did nothing independent of the Father, but He revealed the Father to mankind.** This is the heart of Sonship.

Scripture says that no one has ever seen God except the only Begotten One *who is in the very heart of the Father*. It is from that *intimate* place with the Father that Jesus reveals Him to us (John 1:18). **Only the Son can show us the Father, for the revelation of the Father is *hidden* in the Son, who is hidden in the Father's heart!** And how can we know the Son? Through Holy Spirit whom the Father has sent into our hearts crying, "Abba Father!" Being in Jesus means we are hidden in the Father's heart. This completely counters any fatherless or orphan-spirit thinking.

Abba has given *all* things into the hands of the Son for custody, care, keeping, and judgment, including the intimate knowledge of Himself (John 3:35). Jesus said that no one can know the Son except the Father draws him, and that no one can know the Father except the Son, *and* to whoever the Son *chooses* (*"purposefully, affectionately, and with deliberate desire"*) to reveal the Father (Matt. 11:27).

Think about this for a moment—any revelation of Christ you've been given is because Abba gave it to you. And any revelation of the Father you've received is a purposeful, affectionate, and deliberate act on Jesus' part to show you Abba. And everything comes to us through the activity of the Holy Spirit. This intimate, divine unity can sound dizzying in trying to explain in human words, but it shows the oneness of God *and* what we experience in relationship with God: Father, Son and Holy Spirit.

The divine life *within* us is truly a mystery (Col. 2:2). Spiritual birth cannot be comprehended by the natural mind, because it is a supernatural act of God, one that happens by *His* determination and move of His Spirit, and not by the power of our flesh or another person's desire for us (John 1:13). We may grow up in a Christian home where our parents *desire for* us to be born of God, they take us to Church and teach us Scripture, but it is only the Holy Spirit who can give us new life to be Abba's child in Christ.

THE DOOR TO FATHER'S HOUSE

Most religions teach adherence to rituals and works as the way to gain a deity's approval, but Jesus taught His disciples the way of true life is in *relationship with the Father and the Holy Spirit*. Jesus said, "As the living Father sent Me, and I live because of the Father, so he who feeds on Me, he will also live because of Me" (John 6:57). In other words, Jesus nurtured His entire life on the Father whose very essence became the life force within Jesus. In turn, as we nurture our inner man through relationship with Jesus, the Spirit of the Father becomes our life force too. **We don't flourish in life because we follow a religion, but because we *feed* on the Living *Word* (speech) that comes from the Father, as we have already mentioned.**

The Son is not only the Father's voice sent that we might have life, but He is the DOOR to the Father's house. There is a connection between God's WORD and entrance into His house. In Hebrew, the term *"word"* is *"dabar"* (meaning "speech") and is made of three Hebrew letters: *Dalet, Bet,* and *Resh.* Hebrew letters not only have an assigned sound to them (as languages do), but they also have an assigned picture giving each letter a deeper meaning beyond just a sound. In this case: *Dalet* is the picture of a door; *Bet* is a house, tent, or floor plan; and *Resh* is the picture of a head, meaning: highest, firstborn, or leader. One resource puts these letters together in the following way to give us an understanding of what God's WORD does for us: **"The Word of God serves as the doorway to His home and to participation in His covenant family; those who place Yah's Word above all else, making it top priority, become our Heavenly Father's 'Firstborn' children."**[1]

Jesus is the Word—the fulfillment of all Scripture and prophetic revelation contained within the written Scriptures. He leads us into the Father's house as a covenant family. What's more, is that we not only come in as covenant children because of Christ's covenant with God, but we come in as the *body of the Firstborn.* In Scripture, the firstborn sons belong to God and carry an important leadership position and inheritance. In Christ, the Father actually sees us as firstborn sons, because we are *in* the Firstborn.

Recently, Jesus began speaking to me about the rooms of His Father's house. In my spirit, I saw Him take me in and show me different rooms where different activities take place in Abba's presence—such as Abba's family room where His family interacts and enjoys relationship with one another, and the living room where Father counsels and advises. He showed me Abba's "kitchen," as a place of both sacrifice and delight—sacrifice because what is served is a *life given* to nurture another, and delight because of the rich *life received*. In His house is also a cleansing room for washing, as well as a way to get rid of stuff that we need to let go. There is a place to rest from all other activities, where we can hear Him *speak* to us in a deep and personal way—heart to heart, Spirit to spirit. After this, Jesus reminded me that all these rooms are part of the Tabernacle floor plan given to Moses—it is a pattern of Jesus Himself.

In Abba's house we come to know Father *and* our place in Him. In Christ, we carry a huge weight of leadership and responsibility for doing the Father's will on earth—administering His Kingdom with blessings and authority to prosper the earth. Jesus brings us into the Father's presence for loving the Father as He does, and doing Abba's will on earth with Him. As the body of the Firstborn, we have all the rights and privileges of the Firstborn, and the fullness given to Christ. Let him who has an ear to hear this, hear!

FATHER AFFIRMS HIS SON

As we saw earlier, the affirmation of a father is important to the well-being of a child. It was for Jesus and it is for us too as Abba's children. In Scripture, we see how Jesus openly declared His love for the Father, but also how the Father openly affirmed His love and delight in His Son (Matt. 17:5; John 5:37; 8:18). The Holy Spirit also affirmed Jesus to be the Son of God with power (Rom. 1:4).

This affirmation of Abba Father and Holy Spirit regarding the Son is so important that God's Word says the one who doesn't believe on Jesus as the Son of God is calling *all Three a liar*! (1 John 5:6-12). The Father so honors the Son that He judges how we honor Him too (John 8:49-50). We *cannot* honor Father unless we are honoring His Son.

Scripture says, the one who doesn't honor the Son doesn't honor the Father who sent Him (John 5:22, 23). Jesus didn't glorify Himself, but the Father glorifies Him (John 8:54). The Son's heart beat for one thing—the radiance shared *with His Father* from before the world existed. That glory expressed the intimate unity they share (John 17:5).

Abba not only affirmed Jesus, but confirmed Jesus' coming long before He appeared on earth. Myriad passages (some say over one hundred) in the Old Testament told of His coming, defining where He would be born, what He would be like, and what He would do (see Isa. 7:14; 9:6; Micah 5:2; Zech. 9:9; Ps. 22:16-18 and Isa. 53:3-7 for just a few references). The *Law of Moses* testified of Him, as did the *prophets* (Acts 28:23). Jesus didn't promote Himself, but encouraged those who didn't believe Him regarding His relationship with the Father to at least believe Him for the very *works* that He did—works that glorified the Father (John 5:31; 10:25; 14:11).

While God affirmed Jesus as His Son, the *spirit of the world* hates Him. It hates the very name of Jesus. This is because He came from the Father, who Satan—the god of this world—envies and hates. Jesus said, "Whoever hates Me, hates the Father (John 15:23). Satan introduced sin and rebellion against God to the first Adam, but Jesus (called the "Last Adam") came to destroy Satan's works. Jesus doesn't indulge sin, but calls it for what it is—wickedness against the Father (John 7:7).

Satan's *enmity* against the Father and Son is a spiritual force that seeks to influence cultural systems such as education, media, political policies and cultural ideologies. It works to influence society to be an enemy of God (James 4:4). (This enmity is at the heart of anti-Semitism—the Jews being the line through which Abba sent His Son to us.) But we who are of God, love God and honor Him. Jesus warned us that we are not to be surprised when the world hates us because of our relationship with Him.

The Father affirmed the judgments of the Son, too, because He and the Son are one in judgment (John 8:16). Though Jesus' first coming wasn't to judge but to save, there *is* a judgment by the Son that *is* coming because Abba has committed judgment into the hands of the Son. This is why all humanity is to honor the Son whom the Father sent.

As Abba Father's sons and daughters, it is important for us to fully know that we too are *affirmed* and *supported* by God as His children. He says that His eyes look continually throughout the whole earth to show Himself strong on behalf of those whose heart is completely His (2 Chron. 16:9). He does not send us into the world with a divine commission and then leave us on our own. That is not His nature. His Spirit is *in* us and He is with us, working *through* us as a testimony of His love.

In God's family, each son and daughter is known and affirmed. And one day, we will experience our name honored in heaven as Jesus stands before Father and the angels and declares our name (Rev. 3:5). How marvelous is that!

THE SON'S FREEWILL

The heart of the Son shines with many values, among which are **trust, accountability, freewill and sacrifice**. Jesus said that the Father loves Him because He *willingly* laid down His life so that *we* could have fellowship with the Father (John 10:11-18). No one took Jesus' life from Him; He laid it down on His own initiative, knowing that He had the power and authority to pick His life back up again should He choose to do so. Yes, Jesus had freewill. All humanity does. Yet, in His freewill sacrifice, there was also a deep trust in Jesus toward Abba to not leave Him in a place of death, but to raise Him back to life. Jesus' trust and sacrifice was greatly rewarded. So is ours.

Our Father not only loves His Son, but He loves those who love His Son (John 16:27). This love for the Son is seen through our obedience—it is like a beacon that shines in this dark world, as a city set on a hill (Matt. 12:50; John 14:15). 1 Peter 1:2 says that we are *chosen* by the Father and *sanctified* (*purified, set apart from what is common for a divine use; dedicated to God*) by the Holy Spirit to *obey* the Son who speaks to us the Father's will. Being set apart for God means you are not common—there is a divine purpose for your life.

The Son viewed His life as being *set apart* for the Father's use to bring Him glory (John 10:36; 12:28). Heartfelt obedience is one of the most beautiful expressions of selfless love that a child can give to a parent. When my own children were young, their obedience made my life as a parent so much sweeter! Disobedience, however, brings conflict, division, and hurting hearts on both sides.

Jesus said, "But so that the world may know that I love the Father, I do exactly as the Father commanded Me...."(John 14:31). He was saying that the world sees our love for the Father through our obedience to Him. The very willingness of Jesus to go to the cross in our place, was a unsurpassable act of love for His Father's will. Jesus didn't put conditions on what He would or wouldn't do for His Father. He didn't do only what was convenient or comfortable. He didn't seek what pleased Himself. He embraced Abba's plans even when it meant drinking from a *cup of suffering* (Acts 1:2; John 14:31; 18:11).

In the past, I often wondered why God planned redemption to be through Christ's death on the cross. As a parent, I'd do anything to keep my children from suffering. But one day Father showed me about the greatness of His love for us that would put such a cup of suffering into His Beloved Son's hands. Father used a circumstance our family was going through at the time. Our son was at a place in his life called the *valley of decision*. I knew certain decisions he was about to make could impact his entire future. As he and I engaged in a serious conversation, I stood before my son and, as a parent, I felt an overwhelming sensation that if I could have given my life for him, right then, so that he would choose God's way, I would have done it...without hesitation.

Like all of us, he had made choices in life both wise and unwise. However, I knew this was a critical moment for him. Today, I am grateful that our son chose the path of the Father's design for

115

him. It was in that brief moment, however, that I caught a glimpse of just how much the Father loves us. As a loving Parent Himself, He was willing to give the One He counted most precious over to terrible suffering and death in order to redeem *US* back to Himself. That, my friends, is indescribable love!

Our Heavenly Father didn't throw us away when we fell in darkness. He didn't shrug His shoulders and say, "Oh, well." Instead, He put His plan into action, paying for our return to life with the blood of His Son. No one can tell me that if the Father and Son are one, that Abba didn't intimately experience what Jesus was going through. Abba was not an indifferent onlooker. He didn't send His Son off to war to die alone; Father was *in* Jesus, experiencing His death right there with Him on the cross. He too felt the separation that ripped His Son's heart.

The Father made that *cup of suffering* **(drunk by One) to become the** *cup of blessing* **to be drunk by whosoever will?** (Heb. 2:10; 1 Cor. 10:16) The Son drank that cup to free us from the power of sin and death. He drank it to *rescue us from this present evil age, according to the will of our God and Father"* (Gal. 1:4). In this, Father was, is, and will be glorified by the Son who now sits with Father in heaven (Acts 2:32-33). And not only was the Son raised to life, but so are we.

Just as Jesus *chose* to lay His life down for God's purposes, we too have that freewill choice to serve the Father. The Apostle Paul made that freewill choice and said, "I die *daily"* (1 Cor. 15:31). Paul understood that to walk in divine purpose, the life of the flesh must be laid down. Our freewill sacrifice is a key element to walking in authority in a new life with Christ.

If you are drinking a cup of sorrow right now, I encourage you to continue committing yourself and the situation to the Father. Put your *trust* in Him who loves you, and who is able to make it to become a cup of blessing. Father is able to do abundantly more than what you could ask or think. God promises you victory. Keep your eyes on Him. Trust Him and His timing. God is working. God is faithful. Only wait.

A SON IS NOT FORSAKEN

As a true Son, Jesus did what pleased His Father (John 8:29). Though He *felt* forsaken by all (including God while on the cross), Father was right there with Him (John 16:32). He was there even when others ran away. If Father had forsaken His Son, how could Jesus have committed His spirit into Abba's hands? (Luke 23:46) So why did Jesus cry out, *"My God, My God, why have You forsaken Me?"* Because in bearing our sin, He also experienced the Father's judgment and wrath on that sin.

Sin causes God's face to turn away because sin is the way of Satan—and Jesus felt that separation (Isa. 64:7). Jesus felt *our* separation from God. I can't imagine what that was like for Him to feel. Jesus had only experienced oneness with His Father, but on the cross He experienced the horror, darkness, and abysm of separation from the Father caused by our sin and agreement with evil. He experienced the full weight of sin's penalty for us, that we might experience restoration and oneness with the Father. The Firstborn took upon Himself our sinful state and brought it to the judgment seat of God so that we no longer have to live in that condition.

Abba is a good Father, ever watchful and protective of our destiny. He never forsakes His children. He is committed to us—the cross is His proof. I will never forget God's watchful care and kindness that took me out of darkness—a loveless place that I never want to return to.

THE SON'S ACCOUNTABILITY

As a Son, Jesus held Himself **accountable** to the Father in everything. He saw everything as having come from Father and going back to Father (John 13:3). He held His thoughts and actions accountable to His Father. Accountability is another expression of unity and honor.

God says, "...for those who honor Me I will honor, and those who despise Me will be lightly esteemed" (1 Sam. 2:30). All children, natural and spiritual, must learn accountability for what they have and what they are instructed to do. And as Jesus said,

117

"To whom much is given, much shall be required" (Luke 12:48). Remember, Jesus was given FULLNESS of the Father...that is much! And we have been given that same fullness to be accountable for.

Jesus glorified Father not only by *doing* the work Father gave Him, but by being accountable to *finish* the work given Him (John 16:10; 17:4). And when His work was finished, He returned to the Father who exalted and honored Him. It honors a parent when a son or daughters engages *and* finishes something they are instructed to do. And as with Jesus, there is honor and eternal rewards that await the ones who honor Abba. It's right for a father to have requirements of his children. God is no different. He says we are not to be ignorant, but are to *study* to show ourselves as proven workmen without shame (2 Tim. 2:15). Abba Father has so much for us if we will but walk *humbly* with Him (Micah 6:8).

2   ABBA AND BELIEVERS

In Christ, we are a united family of brothers and sisters who love the Father and the Son. **We share our Father's name "from who every family in heaven and on earth derives its name"** (Eph. 3:14-15). Jesus is called the Firstborn among many brothers and sisters, and He is not ashamed to be called our Brother (Rom. 8:29; Heb. 2:11). He willingly delighted in becoming like us in order to redeem us (Heb. 2:17). He not only treats us as treasured brothers and sisters, but as His intimate friends too. He doesn't see us as mere servants, or as brothers and sisters with whom He cannot relate. He sees us as His friends with whom He can share His heart and Father's plans (John 15:15).

We are viewed by Jesus as the cherished ones that Father has given Him to care for, to whom He reveals the Father's name and keeps us *safe* in that *name* (John 10:27-29; 17:6, 12). "Safe" doesn't necessarily mean the absence of trials or difficulties. What it does mean is that in the midst of life's storms, we are not destroyed. Our Father's name is our place of unceasing help (Ps. 124:8). In the back of this book you will find a list of some of the names of God.

Knowing God's name empowers us as His children. Knowing His name is the source of our strength for taking faith filled action that overcomes the enemy of our soul and advances our Father's Kingdom.

Because of Jesus' *fathering* care for us, He Himself carries the title of "Everlasting Father." He is the delegated protector and place of provision for us as Abba's children (Isa. 9:6). Because of Jesus, we never have to live in the dark regarding our Father's will and purposes for us (John 14:7-9).

A UNITED FAMILY

One of the family dynamics that Jesus shares with us is the importance of unity as a family. Unity glorifies our Father and creates an environment where His blessing is released (John 17:11; Rom. 15:6; Ps. 133). Unity as God's family *and* as Christ's body *is* possible because we have the same indwelling Holy Spirit who pours the love of God into our heart (1 Cor. 12:13-14; Rom. 5:5).

I remember when God began to do a truly transforming work in my life. He not only drew my heart toward Himself, but He dealt with my attitude towards others. God still keeps my heart in check in how I relate to Him *and* to others—He makes sure I am walking in love. In any family, even spiritual families (as with spiritual brothers and sisters in Christ), attitudes and actions are not always perfect. Perceptions can be skewed, actions unloving, and words can be misunderstood as we each learn to walk out our new life in Christ.

Learning a new mindset and way of living is a daily choice.

Earlier I wrote about when earthly families fail, but the truth is that even spiritual families can fail us, and we them. But our Heavenly Father wants us to love one another. As Abba's family, He commands His children to treat one another with love, respect, and honor. He says we are to prefer one another, forgive one another, and esteem one another (Mal. 2:10). If there is dissension, discord, or division, the first thing we should do is check our own heart. We do this by coming to Father and asking Him to examine

119

our heart to see if there is any wicked way operating in us, and then get rid of it! Father wants us to be honest about what's going on inside us, to forgive our brother or sister as He forgives us, and pray for them.

Our Father hates division and strife among His children (Prov. 6:16-19). He says that if we love Him, but do not love our brother, then we are actually walking in darkness and do not know Him (1 John). We can have all the spiritual gifts and wonderful talents and abilities to minister, but if we do not love, we are just clanging cymbals that make a lot of noise (1 Cor. 13:1). In God's family, we are not an "only child." We need one another. Our Father celebrates each one of us and He wants us to celebrate one another.

As Jesus prepared to go to the cross, one of His most important mandates in leaving was His command that His disciples abide in His love, and to love one another (John 15:10-12). The greatest thing a family can do is learn to walk in true love for one another. It's no different with God's family.

As Abba's sons and daughters, we are to pick up our cross and follow Jesus. The cross was not just what Jesus did *for* us to redeem us, but it is the pattern of sacrificial love whereby we love God and one another.

CELEBRATED BROTHERS AND SISTERS

As in any family, each person is unique and special. We each have gift-sets given us with a measure of grace also given by which we are to develop those gifts for benefitting one another. Father wants us to develop uniquely, to celebrate our identity in Him AND celebrate one another—receiving one another as a gift from God.

Abba Father calls us to be *connected* members of His Son's body, not as dismembered body parts, out of fellowship. This enables synergy of the Spirit to operate through a connected "supply" from God that not only matures the body of Christ, but brings divine supply to our communities and the nations (Eph. 4:16). It also pleases the Father's heart.

A FAMILY OF ONE SPIRIT

As Abba's children, we no longer have the *spirit of the world* driving or guiding us, but we have the *Spirit of God* filling us and leading us, so that we can freely know the things of our Father and walk in them (1 Cor. 2:12). We are a family—one body, one Spirit, one Lord, one Father (1 Cor. 6:17; Eph. 4:4-6).

Just as Jesus had the unlimited presence of the Holy Spirit, in Him we do too. We are born of the Spirit, and are baptized of the Spirit. We have the same anointing to heal the sick, open blind eyes, cast out demons, and bring freedom to people who are in captivity. We have the same access to the Father by the Spirit that Jesus had while on earth (John 3:34; Eph. 2:18).

The Holy Spirit teaches us the mysteries of God. He searches the depths and thoughts of God, and shows them to us. He reveals the things of the Father and Son to us so that we can walk empowered as God's sons and daughters (1 Cor. 2:9-11). As mentioned earlier, the Holy Spirit testifies about the Son to us and reminds us of His words (John 14:26; 15:26-27). He speaks words of encouragement, wisdom, counsel, revelation, and knowledge to us, and to us for others. He inspires our heart and the gifts within us for effective service. The Spirit fills us with boldness to co-labor with Jesus in ministering the Father's Kingdom.

The Holy Spirit moves us to speak to others of Jesus (John 16:12-13). He is the fire within us that motivates us as Abba's sons and daughters to go and teach all nations everything that Jesus has said (Matt. 28:19). Father wants us to take that blessing and let it shine with radiance, so that *all* men come to the knowledge of the truth in the Son, and be saved (Matt. 5:14). Abba Father wants many more sons and daughters who know His love!

A FAMILY OF TRUTH

God is truth, Jesus is truth, and the Holy Spirit is the Spirit of truth—we are a family of truth. Truth is power and freedom. Not free as being lawless, but free to truly love. Not power as tyranny, but as having authority and being rescued from powerless living. We are not longer orphans trying to find our way, but we are fa-

121

thered by God, and tutored by the Holy Spirit for living as His children.

To walk with our Heavenly Father, we must walk and worship Him in Spirit and in Truth. It is in this relationship that we flourish in what Abba says of us as being: *"the display of His manifold wisdom before principalities and powers in the heavens"* (Eph. 3:10). What a powerful view our Father has of us as His children.

3 ABBA AND ISRAEL

I cannot end this chapter without also speaking about Israel, though this topic is a book in itself. I will be brief and encourage you to read God's Word about Israel and interpret it with His fathering heart toward His much loved son.

Our God and Father formed Israel as both a son and as a bride for Himself (Ex. 4:22; Hos. 2:6). Israel was chosen as a nation to be carriers of divine light and the truths of God. It was through Israel that our Father chose to bring forth the world's Messiah—Jesus.

Scripture teaches that it is Israel "to whom belongs the adoption as sons, and the glory and the covenant and the giving of the Law and the temple service and the promises, whose are the fathers, and from whom is the Christ according to the flesh, who is over all" (Rom. 9:4-5). Through Israel, our Father gave us the foundation and fullness of our salvation—Christ Himself who brings us near to God. God made Israel to be a guardian of His divine revelations.

The anti-Semitism we see today is the manifestation of hatred not just against Israel, but against the Father and covenant of adoption. Though Israel has been wayward and blind regarding the full purposes of the Father, even rejecting the Mediator of the covenant given them (Yeshua), Israel is still loved deeply by the Father who brought Israel into existence. Everything that concerns Israel is a matter of concern to Abba Father (Jer. 31:9).

God's covenant with Israel has never ceased, rather it transitioned from one mediator, *Moses and the law,* to Christ who fulfilled the law (Jer. 31:31-33; Heb. 8:8-13). The New Covenant that we enjoy is one that Israel was given from the Father and into which we are grafted as adopted sons (Rom. 11:1-5). Though they hold the covenant, not all Israel has entered into the covenant through the Mediator sent from Father.

We must be clear that Father did not take away His covenant from Israel in order to give it to the world. Our Father doesn't take back His gifts; the New Covenant is still theirs from Him. Again, we are grafted into the covenant God gave them in Yeshua. However, as with any gift, one has the choice to receive it, or not. God used Israel's blindness to bring the whole world back — whoever believes — into relationship with Himself through Jesus' sacrifice. Though Israel's eyes have been blind to the truths they have been chosen to guard, there is a fresh move of the Holy Spirit in Israel today, and even worldwide, and many Jews are receiving Abba's New Covenant in Yeshua (Rev. 1:7).

Replacement theology grieves the Father's heart and we must remove every root of it from our doctrines and mindsets. It is a doctrine of demons and should have NO place in us as Abba's sons and daughters. Israel's history is full of our fathers of faith — fathers who have written for us God's truths and divine revelations from Him. To reject current Israel is to not see the destiny that our Father still sees for them.

Just because Israel, as a nation, rejected the Mediator of God's New Covenant with them, does not negate the truth that it was given to them and is still with them, whether they realize it or not...whether the world as a family of humanity understands it or not. God still loves His son, Israel.

Father's faithfulness to Israel stands as an ensign of His faithfulness to us. **God does not forsake or abandon His children.** He still loves Israel, and as a true Father He will never throw His son away (read Hosea). It is up to wayward sons to return home to Father's open arms. Abba is a good Father; He is for Israel and with Israel, just as He is with us. He doesn't leave Israel, lose him, forget him, or disown him. God will work to perfect what He has begun in His sons, including Israel, until Jesus' return (Phil. 1:6). It is the promise of covenant.

It is important for us to realize that Father Himself also gave to His son, Israel, the land where they are now occupying as an inheritance (Gen. 13:15, 17; 15:18; Josh. 21:43). He didn't take that away either. It belongs to Israel no matter who else tries to claim it. It is the place where the God of Israel — the *King of Glory* — will soon return to set up His reign. Israel belongs to God, and His eyes are continually on that *land* as *His* own (Deut. 11:12; 33:13). No wonder there is so much war over that small area of soil — it is a *spiritual warfare* between the will of God and Satan's desire to take what belongs to God. We know who wins. Let us side with the Champion of Battle!

Abba Father, thank You for Jesus. Thank You for family, natural and spiritual. And thank You for Israel. Teach us to love our families and Israel as You do.

PERSONAL APPLICATION:
1. Do you desire to please the Father? In what ways?
2. What is the "patternicity" of your thought-life like?
3. Do you feel affirmed by Abba Father? Why or why not?
4. In what ways do you honor the Son?
5. Do you feel accountable to the Father for the life and call He has given you?
6. In what ways are you revealing the Father to others?
7. How healthy is your "family life" with other believers? Do you find unity with the body of Christ easy or difficult? Why or why not?
8. How do you feel about Israel?

CHAPTER 8

ABBA FATHER *and* YOU

"My father taught me that the easiest thing to do was to quit.
He'd say, 'It doesn't take any talent to do that.'"
— Ken Venturi [1]

Abba Father wants us to see Him as being involved in every area of our lives. 1 Peter 5:7 says that God cares *for* us. Some times we interpret that to mean He cares *about* us, but it means what it says—He cares *for* us. As our Father, He takes seriously His charge of our wellbeing.

No doubt, we have all gone through times when we've thought, *"Where are You, God? Do you really care what I'm going through? Do You see? Do You have a plan for my life?"* We want to experience the reality of our theology regarding His care and involvement. We want to know Him and see Him in our circumstance. We want to experience His participation with us, and not feel that He is simply watching from afar.

One time I was rehearsing the *"why"* question to God about a loss I was going through. I was whining and questioning His care, when I heard Him say, *"How can I not care, or know how you feel, or be intimately involved with you when My Holy Spirit lives in you?"* As I meditated on the impact of His words to me, I realized that if the Father, Son, and Holy Spirit are intimately One, then how can Father not be intimately involved with the Body of His Son (you and me) in whom His Spirit dwells? I determined that it would be *impossible*!

During another time when "storm winds" rushed in on multiple fronts of my life, I was having trouble sleeping. One particular night my mind was wrestling with a number of sudden changes. I had finally dozed off to sleep, but in the night I awoke to hearing the word, "*Elroi.*" I immediately thought of the story of Hagar, and I knew God was speaking to me. I looked at my clock; it was 2:00 a.m. I was tired, but I wanted to know what God was saying. So I got up, went to the kitchen, sat at the table, opened my Bible, and turned to Genesis 16. There I read about Hagar running away from a painful circumstance. Nevertheless, God put Himself in Hagar's path and let her know — "*I see what you're going through!*"

God revealed Himself to Hagar as "*Elroi,*" which means: "*the God who sees me.*" Not only did God let her know that He saw her circumstance, but He gave her counsel, direction, and a promise. He saw, He cared, and He provided what she needed in the midst of a personal storm.

These are things God wants us to have as we meet with Him in the midst of our circumstances. For Hagar, God's counsel was for her to go back and submit to the authority over her. Hagar put her trust in God and did as He said. I knew that God was also telling me to do the same.

Father wants us to put our trust in Him and look to Him in everything. He will tell us what we need to know and what to do. He sees and cares for us right where we are, using all things to shape our life for His purposes and for the destiny we carry. His care and power has granted us everything we need for life and godliness regarding the *identity* we carry as His sons and daughters (2 Pet. 1:3).

ABBA'S PROVISION

Our Father supplies unlimited provision for us through covenant in Christ. The legal document of His covenant with us was signed with Jesus' own blood. In God's Word, covenants were a pact, a bond of loyal friendship between two parties. Covenants provided needed supply, aid, and protection—all that one had—for the help and benefit of the other. It even included taking on the debt of the other party as needed.

Jesus' blood paid our full debt on the cross—a debt we could never pay. We don't "owe" God anything in order to be righteous before Him. Salvation is a free gift. Yet, love compels us to give Him everything that we have, and are. When we truly see the great price He paid, we will love Him much, because we know that we have been forgiven much.

The book of Psalms contains endless testimony of what God provides for us as His children. Psalm 103 says that He *forgives* all our iniquities, *heals* all our diseases, *redeems* our life from the pit, *crowns* us with lovingkindness, *satisfies* our years with good things, *renews* our strength, *releases* justice for the oppressed, *teaches* us His ways, and does not deal with us according to our sins, but *removes* them from us as far as the east is from the west.

Psalm 103:13 says that *as a father has compassion on his children, so the Lord has compassion on those who fear Him.* The word "compassion" (Heb. *"racham"*) means: to love deeply with tender affection, to pity, to cherish, to treat gently. Our Father is tender toward us right where we're at in life. He is not stingy, but provides—for *all* who look to Him—out of the infinite abundance of His grace. He blesses *richly* all who call on Him (Rom. 10:12; Eph. 2:7).

Psalm 104 continues saying how He *makes angels His messengers* to us, makes a *way* for us, *sets boundaries*, sends waters to *refresh* and bring *increase*, provides *food,* and sends His Spirit to *renew* the land. That sounds pretty involved if you ask me...and His provision is endless!

Abba promises to give needed supply out of the vastness of His wealth made available to us *in Christ* (Phil. 4:19). **In other words, our *source* of provision does not spring *from* the earth realm, but comes *from* the unseen realm of Father's Kingdom—even if it comes *through* human or natural agents** (Heb. 11:3).

127

Remember how Jesus supplied food for the multitudes? (Matt. 14:19). Or how God supplied manna in the wilderness? (Exod. 16:15). Remember the wind that made a way for Israel to cross the Red Sea? (Exod. 14:21). Or the earthquake that set Paul and Silas free from the prison house as they were praising? (Acts 16:25-26). Our Father has unlimited supply *and* ways to provide for our every need.

Abba Father is not too busy for us, distant, distracted, or indifferent towards us. In fact, He sees *before* we ask (Matt. 6:8, 32). He says, *"Don't worry about what you're going to eat, drink, or wear. I'll take care of you. The very birds of the air eat what I provide through the hands of another. They don't worry; they just accept what I provide and how I provide for them. Aren't you more important to Me than they are? I think you are!"* (Matt. 6:26-28 — my version).

Difficult circumstances can make us feel desperate. Father says that if even the wicked know how to give good gifts to their children, how much more will He give good things to those who ask Him, especially food and shelter (Matt. 7:11). The Father wants us to trust Him for what we need.

During the time of first writing this book, my husband was out of work for many months. The morning after he received the "pink slip," I was just rousing from sleep, though not yet fully awake, when I had a vision in my spirit as follows: I was looking toward the heavens and was aware that *God in heaven was speaking,* when suddenly a small red bird *appeared in front of me.* It was quite comical, like something you would see in a cartoon — the bird appeared as a magical "poof" and there he was! I sat up, fully awake, and I knew what God was saying. **He was letting me know that our provision would certainly manifest in the natural, but it would come from Him.** Our expectation was to be in Him and His word.

Abba Father provides for our needs — spirit, soul, and body — in the midst of *every* situation (Eph. 3:16). Remember what we looked at earlier in how we are dependent on Father's voice. He will supply in ways we would never even think of (Matt. 4:4; John

6:32). His provision comes as finances, food, employment, and shelter, as well as wisdom and revelation. We are spirit *and* natural beings and He cares about *all* of who we are. This is why true ministry begins with taking care of the fatherless, widows, and the poor as we preach the gospel, heal the sick and cast out demons. We are to minister the power and love of God to the whole man, just as He ministers and provides for us. Our *whole* life is valuable to God.

Abba Father gives us so much; He supplies us with a ceaseless hope and **expectation** and strengthens our hearts in *all* things (2 Thess. 2:16, 17). He equips us for sharing in a great inheritance *in* light (Col. 1:12). He does this by the work of the Spirit and the Son in us to make us fit and *suitable for eternal glory;* His grace makes us *suitable heirs together* under one Father **from** whom all things come, one Lord **through** whom all things come, and one Spirit **by** whom all things come (1 Cor. 8:6). What a fantastic provision we have!

ABBA IS A SAFE FATHER

Our Heavenly Father is not only good to provide for us, but He is a *safe* Father. Because of what some have negatively experienced from an earthly father, this is an important truth to grasp. He is strong, but He is a place of safety for His children...and He is a safe Father. Let's look.

Psalm 78:53 says, "He led them **safely**, so that they did not fear; but the sea engulfed their enemies." Abba Father doesn't treat us harshly or go into a rage when we do something wrong. He is not emotionally unsafe. He doesn't yell at or beat His children. That is not His nature. We've already noted His own description of Himself in being gentle, patient, and slow to anger. However, while He is forgiving, He also says that the guilty will not go unpunished. He is a just God. His justice is right and true, and is not chaotic and unjust as with the wicked.

Though there is a *day of wrath* coming where judgment will manifest on the wicked, God's holy anger is righteous and **fore-**

warned as He gives every opportunity possible for a person or people group to change before His wrath is revealed. There *is* a righteous anger of God—He can be violent against His enemies and those who dishonor His Son. Nevertheless, He is not impulsive, moody, or uncontrolled, nor does He act in fist-flailing hostility, especially toward His children.

God is not a brawler, but then neither is He a "push-over." He doesn't act rashly or rude, nor does He discipline as such. Slapping, yelling, and name calling to change another's behavior is a destructive reality in many homes. This is not Father's way. It is not honorable. It is not love. It does not produce righteousness, and teaches a child that the home is unsafe, and that discipline has no purpose other than to inflict punishment, or release a parent's own anger and frustration. That is how people act, not God.

If "unsafe hands" was your reality growing up, Abba Father wants to heal that wound, right now. Go to Him about it. Talk to Him. Receive His love. Let Him heal your heart as you choose to forgive whoever has wounded you and commit them into God's hands.

While Abba is a Father who disciplines us, He does so in *love*, not in anger. As a Father, He charges all earthly fathers to correct their children, but *never* in anger (Eph. 6:4). Unsafe actions of earthly parents can lay a wrong foundation in our concept of God, and make us fear Him as being emotionally unsafe too. We jokingly says, *"God's lightening is going to strike us,"* but too often it reflects how we really see Him.

A parent may deeply love their child, but unsafe emotions sends another message. Fear promotes a feeling of being unsafe, triggering a "fight or flight" response in us. While we *are* to reverence God and tremble at His Word, it is a fear that is rooted in deep respect and love that compels us to humble ourselves, heed His words, and run *to* Him for cleansing and help. It is not a dread that makes His children feel like running away. Holy fear encourages us to draw near to God, knowing that He loves us and is bigger than any difficulty we face or weakness we have.

Our Father is supremely just and sovereign in power, yet He is also intrinsically kind and merciful in heart.

As we learn to trust His care, seeing how He stoops low to help us, *unrighteous* fear is removed. **Abba wants us to believe in His loving care when our world is shaken.** Fear, worry, and anxiety operate *apart* from His love, but Father's perfect love drives out fear (1 John 4:18). If you feel anxious, talk to God about it. Ask Him to show you the root of it.

While God *is* a Man of War, He is not a "violent man." As we've seen, our Champion in Battle fights for what is right and upholds justice. A violent man is one who rages against others out of wickedness and an evil heart. As a Man of War, Father protects what is His—**we are His!** He shows Himself strong on the behalf of those who love Him (Deut. 1:30-32).

When we know our Father's thoughts and nature toward us, we will live from that reality and perspective. Jesus trusted the Father implicitly, He was confident in Abba's love. He knew that if He asked, Father would have sent twelve legions of angels to save Him from the cup of suffering (Mat. 26:53).

We may not understand the "why" of things we go through, but Father wants us to trust Him and not shrink back in the midst of difficulties. He will carry us *through* our wildernesses and He will bring us *out* into larger realms, planting us on higher places (Ps. 68:9). It is His promise.

A JOYFUL FATHER

Our Father and His Kingdom is a joyful place. King David discovered that in His presence is *fullness of joy* with unceasing pleasures (Ps. 16:11). The very manifestation of His Spirit is joy (Gal. 5:22). Jesus Himself was anointed with joy (Heb. 1:9). So there we have it—the Holy Trinity is joyful!

There is an unexplainable pleasure in God's presence. People seek pleasure in all kinds of ways, some good and some bad. God seeks pleasure! It's why He made us. And we are made to know pleasure too. I have seen people be so overwhelmed by the presence of God's joy, it was as if they were drunk. I have experienced it myself. The early Church experienced it too. In fact, the Church of power began with 120 people experiencing the joy of the Holy Spirit as they were baptized in the Spirit with holy fire (Acts 2). People on the streets saw them and thought they were drunk!

Psalm 89:15 tells us that those who "know the joyful sound" are a blessed people who walk in the light of God's face. Isaiah 64:5 says that God *meets* with him who *rejoices* and does righteousness. He says His people "rejoice all day in His name" (Ps. 89:16). As a parent, I too want my kids to be joyful, not sad, depressed, fearful, or gloomy.

I once had a pastor tell me that God doesn't want people happy, just faithful. Though I believe Father wants His children to be faithful, I don't agree that He doesn't care about our joy, especially when He tells us to rejoice!

As Abba's sons and daughters we have been given the mind of Christ—one that is full of joy and peace (1 Cor. 2:16). Like the prophet of old declared, God's joy is our strength (Neh. 8:10).

FATHER KEEPS HIS PROMISES

Some people fail to follow through with what they say, but Father always keeps His word (2 Pet. 3:9). He keeps His promises. Most everyone has been impacted by unfulfilled promises made by earthly parents or leaders, but our Father actually *watches over His Word to perform it* (Jer. 1:12). His own zeal accomplishes His Word—He is excited about seeing it come to pass (Isa. 9:7).

Father *loves processes*, and most often His words require time. His timing, however, is perfect. He wants us to rest in that understanding. Too many times we expect Father to fulfill a promise exactly how and when *we* think it should happen.

Look at the dream that Joseph had of his own father, mother, and eleven brothers all bowing down to him (Gen. 37:9-10). The reality was that Joseph's mother had already died when his prophetic dream came to pass. But the purpose of the dream wasn't about her, but about God's plan for Joseph and how he would become a ruler and provider for many, including his family.

All of God's promises are "yes and amen," but we must also let Him work them out the way He wants to. As we learn to let Him interpret what He says, we won't be set up for disillusionment, discouragement, and unfulfilled expectations. Our part is to simply obey what He has been saying to us, and rest our expectation in God and His Word, and not in what the circumstances look like. Father is faithful and He will perform all His good work (Phil. 1:6).

Fulfillment of promises may not always look like what we think, but with God, it will always be good! He is always working something out, so He wants us to enjoy the journey—listening and doing what He tells us, and He will do the rest (Luke 24:49). Father knows our end from our beginning and is sovereign in *how* He fulfills His Word to us.

FATHER ACTIVELY LISTENS TO US

One of the most important tools of good parenting is good listening. While parents often ask their children, "Did you hear me?" they themselves often have a listening problem. I know by experience!

When children are small, it is easy to "tune-them-out" with all their chatter, endless questions, and "I wants." When my children were young, they realized my habit of sometimes tuning-them-out and they would occasionally make a game of it.

One day, they came and stood beside me while I was reading a book and said, "We're going to take the car and drive to Disneyworld now." Not paying attention, I nodded and responded, "Uh-huh, okay, that's fine." To which they responded, "Great, bye!" I realized what was just said and we all burst out laughing at how I'd just given permission to an 8 and 9 year old to make a 900 mile trip on their own . . . in my car!

While that scene is laughable, sometimes the habit of "tuning-out" a child becomes a lack of awareness as to what is really going on with our children. Being *unaware* means lack of action. But our Father who says to watch and pray is Himself *always* alert to us.

Abba Father has keen listening skills. He hears even when we don't want Him to (like when we're complaining). He hears our thoughts before we even speak. He hears our prayers and He answers us (Ps. 65:2). People may tune us out, but Father God does not tune us out.

Things our Father hears:

- He hears our grieving (Jer. 31:8)
- He hears our prayers and sees our tears (2 Kings 20:5)
- He hears our groaning in bondage (Exod. 6:5)
- He hears our cry for help (2 Sam. 22:7)
- He hears our words (Dan. 10:12)
- He hears our complaining (Exod. 16:12)

King David lived in the confidence of knowing that God heard his prayers. This encouraged him to continually look to God for help *with* an expectation of His response (Ps. 40:1; 116:2). Abba Father wants you and I to live in the confidence that He is attentive to us, and that when we ask, He will answer. He doesn't drop everything at our beck and call, but He promises, "**Ask, and it *will* be given you; seek and you *will* find; knock, and it *will* be opened to you**" (Matt. 7:7, emphasis mine).

As children, we need to have patience. Too often the experience of feeling not heard or listened to by parents or leaders makes us think God is that way, too. But God is not a human being, and we must not treat Him as such. If we are waiting for some needed answer, there is a reason. Keep confident and keep in prayer. Sometimes He doesn't always tell us *why* at the moment, but He *is* a good Father and will speak to us. He will also work things out as we pray and look to Him for the answer to our needs.

Jesus taught those who followed Him to be confident in the Father's involvement with them saying, "Whatever you ask in the

Son's name, Father will give it to you" (John 16:23). The Apostle John said, **"This is the confidence which we have before Him, that if we ask anything according to His will, He hears us. And if we know that He hears us in whatever we ask, we know that we have the requests which we have asked from Him"** (1 John 5:14-15).

God also gives a promise that when two are in prayerful agreement regarding His will, He hears us (Matt. 18:19).

Here are a few ways that increase our ability to receive answers from Father:

- All things are possible to him who *prays* and *believes* (Matt. 21:22; Mark 11:24)
- *Abiding* in Jesus and His Words (John 15:7)
- Walking in *forgiveness* (Mark 11:25-26)
- *Asking* with right motives (James 4:2-3)
- *Praying* according to His will (1 John 5:14-15)
- *Treating* our spouse with love (1 Pet. 3:7)

Jesus was confident that Father *always* heard Him (John 11:41-42). Jesus didn't say that Father jumped to answer His every whim, but He trusted Abba knowing that Father always actively heard Him and would answer. And so, Jesus thanked Him before He even saw the answer appear.

Practicing gratitude for all Father *has* done helps keep our heart in a place of faith while we wait on His perfect timing for answers. Even when King David expressed his honest pain about things happening in his life, he always ended his dialogue with trust.

It grieves a parent when a child expresses distrust in a parent's care or disbelief in a parent's words, especially for a father or mother who cares deeply for the wellbeing of that child. It grieves Abba Father when we mistrust His care and disbelieve His words. Our complaining may easily carry an accusation toward Him regarding His motives in caring for us. Abba Father doesn't want us to ignore our feelings, or put on a fake smile, but He wants us to address them honestly, identify their motive and source, and know that He cares and will help us. He wants to hear how we feel *and* that we trust Him (1 Thess. 5:18). Gratitude expresses trust that Father is *actively* listening.

LISTENING TO OUR FATHER

When we are born into this world we are given physical attributes that enable us to interact with this world: vision, hearing, smell, touch, and taste. It is the same when we are born of God—we are given *spiritual* senses of vision, hearing, discernment, touch (experiential knowledge), and taste—capacities by which we experience the spiritual world. Abba Father wants us to use all these senses. Scripture talks a lot about hearing God as an especially important aspect of our family life with God and interaction with Him.

As His child, we are born with great privilege for a great purpose. We have a new culture to learn, and a new way of doing life with intentionality. Ears that were once deaf to God are reawakened and we have to learn to pay attention to our Father's words.

It is a mark of maturity when we listen attentively to Father's instructions...and *do* them.

The impact of God's voice in our life is linked to the way we listen to Him. A listening ear and heart that obeys shapes our life into one of faith and power. Our formation as His child is so important that He gave us a whole book specifically on the importance of *listening* to instruction: the book of Proverbs.

In Proverbs we read how Wisdom is like a woman who stands at the top of the street calling to us, "Listen to Me and you shall live!"

We have been given ears for hearing God, but listening is a choice. And even when we listen, there are different *ways* we listen.

Here are a few of the ways we listen:

- **Passive listening** (we hear but do not obey, or delay obedience)

- **Selective listening** (we listen with bias or for what we want to hear)

- **Inattentive listening** (we focus in and out of the conversation)

- **Attentive listening** (we seek to hear and understand, and *take action*)

Any other form of listening other than attentive, is *not really* listening.

FATHER'S INSTRUCTION MANUAL

The Word of God is our instruction book for life. It's why I have included Scripture references for you throughout this book—to show you that the words I'm sharing are not my own opinion, but God's revealed truth. God's Word teaches us about His character, ways, and purpose. While Abba instructs us through His written *and* spoken Word, His *voice* will *always* be consistent with what is in His written Word.

Knowing the Bible intimately helps us to know if what we hear in our *inner man* or thoughts is God, or not, and is consistent with His nature and purposes, or not. Following a voice or thought that is contrary to God's written Word is what leads us into all kinds of error. *Attentive* listening to His voice teaches us what His voice sounds like.

Other ways that God speaks to us include, a word we hear in our spirit-man, a thought, an impression, a picture in our spirit, or even a physical sensation, or a sense of knowing something. He uses our feelings, and even colors and smells as ways to convey His thoughts to us. He uses people, parents, friends, leaders, circumstances, books, music, dreams, visions, creation, and *His* angels, plus more. God speaks to us in countless ways, but again, *always consistent with His written Word.*

Jesus listened attentively to the Father and only spoke what He heard from Him, so listening to Jesus is also listening to Father. The Holy Spirit also speaks (John 16:13). *God is a speaking God.*

The question is then: What is He saying? Are we listening?

137

RESPONDING TO OUR FATHER'S WORDS

Listening is an act of love. Doing is also an act of love. According to our Father, **listening is completed by *doing*.** If we don't *do* what we hear, then we haven't really heard. And if we don't listen and do, then we haven't learned to fully love. Pleasures, self-will, and distractions are all things that a child must be trained to hold as less important than a parent's instruction. It is the same for us regarding Father's voice. Following our desires above Father's words is what plummeted mankind into darkness—the place we have been translated *out of*.

The success of our development as sons and daughters of God rests on love that listens to and follows divine instruction.

As earthly parents, it's easy to unknowingly cultivate the self-centered nature of our children. We do this through over permissiveness or by allowing the child to obey when it is convenient for *them*. Parenting isn't easy and sometimes we work hard to find the right way to discipline, but when we allow them to decide the time and way in which they do chores or responsibilities, it teaches them that *their desires* are greater than parental instruction. And we all know what they say: "Give 'em an inch and they'll take a mile." A child's *"just a minute"* becomes *"later,"* and *"later"* becomes *"tomorrow."* And, as we know, tomorrow never comes.

How often do we do that with Father God? Are we acting on what He is saying? Or do we say, "Just a minute"...or perhaps the "later" that never comes? What do our actions show to be more important to us—our desires or Father's?

Catering to a child's timetable establishes the hierarchy of a child's self-will. There is nothing that robs us more of victory in life and destiny in God, than *self*-will. Sometimes, however, it isn't self-will that keeps us from hearing Father, but busyness, distraction, and even the voice of emotional turmoil. Peace is important for our ability to receive direction from God.

Peace is the ambient in which we best hear Father's voice and receive divine revelation. No wonder Father sent Jesus as the

Prince of Peace. Satan works to keep us out of peace; focusing our trust in God in all things keeps us in perfect peace (Isa. 26:3). The Apostle Peter said to seek peace and *run after* it! (1 Pet. 3:11). Make it a priority for the health and wholeness of your mind and life!

THE REWARD OF ACTION

What is the voice you are hearing right now? Your own? The enemy? Circumstances? The Holy Spirit? It is important to discern and pay attention to what we are listening to. If it's right instruction we are to follow it; if it's wrong thoughts we are to capture them and bring them into the obedience of Christ. We have been given a wonderful God-given ability to overcome in life. Words and thoughts that spring from the spirit of this world, our carnal nature, or demonic presence produce death in us, but God's voice produces life and joy (John 8:38, 44).

The book of Proverbs teaches us that a child who refuses instruction reaps personal destruction, and a child who lightly esteems (dishonors, disgraces, or treats shamefully) a parent's instructions reaps *curses* (afflictions, condemnation, and evil) upon their life. That is *not* joy. God says that one day that child will say, "Woe is me because I have hated instruction and spurned my teachers" (Deut. 27:16; Prov. 5). How important it is for us to embrace wise instruction, and even more important, Abba Father's instruction that shapes our purpose and destiny.

Father honors the one who honors Him and His words. He has given us His Spirit to be our Teacher so that we know His words and act on them. Embracing His instruction and wisdom brings *blessing* to our life. Proverbs 4:9 says that wisdom crowns us with honor as when someone wins an Olympic game. Paul said that life is a race, and we are to run in such a way as to win. So let's listen! Let's run! Let's Win!

RECEIVING FATHER'S COUNSEL

Instruction and counsel are similar yet different. By definition, *instruction* is information, teaching, and knowledge given as direc-

139

tion or command; *counsel* is instruction, yet as a *recommendation* given *upon request,* or as an *exhortation* or *warning.* We tend to seek counsel when we need advice in a specific circumstance or area. We ask, *"Dad, what do I do now, in this moment of time?"*

Isaiah 58:11 says that His *daily* counsel will satisfy us in times of drought and make us like a flourishing garden with a spring that never goes dry.

In Revelation 3:18, Jesus *counseled* the church of Laodicea to buy of Him *"gold that is tried in the fire."* The church appeared to be a fellowship of "good Christians" with good works, but God saw their hearts as being indifferent toward Him, and they were in danger of His judgments. God sees areas where we are blind and in need of counsel. In the Old Testament, one of God's greatest issues with Israel was their constant waywardness as *"a nation lacking in counsel and without understanding"* (Deut. 32:28-29). Their heart was indifferent toward Him.

Abba's counsel makes us wise and enables us to *see* the future He has for us, helping to us know the way we should go (1 Thess. 3:11). Living without His instruction *and* counsel leads to our making choices without His wisdom. This negatively impacts our present success and ability to understand and discern the days ahead. God counsels and instructs us so that we are a people who know what God is doing, so that we move with Him accordingly.

The children of Israel knew how to honor earthly fathers, but neglected to honor their Heavenly Father. They were called to be a nation of faithful priests who carried God's glory, but their heart wanted to be like the rest of the nations, so they turned away from Him to serve other gods—*their heart ran away from Home.* In rejecting knowledge, their eyes became blind regarding the future that awaits those who forget God. Worldly pursuit made them ignorant and foolish; they abdicated their divine call.

Nevertheless, God didn't forsake Israel, but continually called them to turn from their waywardness and return to understand their divine destiny. He is still calling Israel. So too, Father calls us to come out of our waywardness and not to be like the rest of the

Abba Father and You

nations. We are a royal and priestly people created for governing this world. God is a Father waiting for His children to come home and take their place with Him.

Psalm 32:8 says, "I will instruct [give insight to] you and teach you in the way which you should go; I will counsel [advise, purpose] you with My eye upon you" (Amplified Bible).

THE SPIRIT OF COUNSEL

As Abba's sons, we have been given the *Spirit of Counsel*. Refusing to listen to His counsel grieves His heart and quenches the work of His Spirit. To this He says, "Do not quench the Spirit!" — do not extinguish, suppress, or stifle the fire of divine influence! (1 Thess. 5:19). No one likes to be ignored, especially someone with whom we are in intimate relationship with. How much more God doesn't like to be ignored!

God is patient with us, but He has much better plans for us than to be continually calling us out of sin and unbelief! He wants us to move forward into His promises and possess the inheritance He has given us. He calls us to run with *Him*, not after the world.

Proverbs 8:34 says, "Blessed is the man who listens to Me, watching daily at My gates." As the body of Christ, we are the royal priests of God; it is the duty of kings to govern wisely and the duty of priests is to live in intimacy with God — meeting with Him, and moving at His counsel. (Exod. 30:6).

Proverbs 8:14-15 says that **counsel is found in the fear of the Lord and by it kings reign.** *We are kings* who have been appointed our Father's Kingdom, and it is His counsel that causes us to prosper and be victorious in battle (Luke 22:29; Judg. 18:5; 20:18, 23). When we receive Father's counsel and speak it into our homes, businesses, or other spheres of influence, God's power is released into those places to bring increase, order, restoration and healing. Environments are shifted as we hear and release God's words of authority and power.

Abba Father has a glorious plan for our present and future, and it can only be known through seeking and listening to His strate-

141

gic counsel and instruction. Satan doesn't want us to engage with God's counsel because He knows it is *our* victory and *his* defeat.

AGREEMENT WITH OUR FATHER

We are in the last days and there is a great shaking already beginning in the earth. Nation will rise against nation and natural disasters will increase. Persecution and offenses will abound and cultures will be in tumult. Gross darkness and deception will cover the earth, and people will fear. Scripture says that people will be lovers of themselves and of money; they will be proud, disobedient, ungrateful, unholy, unloving, and loving pleasure rather than loving God. They will hold to a form of religion that has no power (Matt. 24; 2 Tim. 3:1-7; Isa. 60:2).

Nevertheless, something else has also been promised for the last days, too! It is the outpouring of His Holy Spirit upon His sons and daughters. God's children will see visions, dream dreams, and prophesy (Acts 2:17; Hab. 2:14). They will move in the power of His Spirit and His counsel and do exploits. God's glory will be on His people who love Him and who take confident refuge in Him, and not run after the world (Prov. 14:26).

As sons and daughters of God, we must break every *inward* tie to worldly systems and be governed by the counsel of God. Our thinking must be rooted in the Kingdom of heaven, and not in the kingdoms of this world. As we seek Abba's counsel, He will show us what we are to do. In the Old Testament, as God's people *listened* to Him and *loved* Him (and not idols), they prospered...even in times of famine.

Abba Father desires for you and me to prosper, advance, and move with Him in divine purpose for the world around us. He wants you and I to be confident in His provision, rest in His love, and listen to what He is saying, and take action. There are people all around us who are meant to be touched with the words and power of God through us. May we step fully, unhindered, into our high calling as Abba Father's children.

Father, help us to see You for who You really are, to know that You care for us and listen to us. Help us to listen to You intentionally and embrace Your counsel as wise children. Teach us agreement with You.

PERSONAL APPLICATION:

1. In what ways do you see Father's provision in your life?
2. Do you see Father God as safe? Why or why not?
3. What are some of Father's promises to you? Which ones have you seen fulfilled?
4. Do you feel that Father listens to you?
5. Do you feel that you listen to Father?
6. What was the last counsel that Father gave you?
7. Did you act on what He told you? In what ways?

CHAPTER 9

ABBA'S DISCIPLINE

*"My Son, do not reject the discipline of the Lord or
loathe His reproof, for whom the Lord loves He reproves, even as a Father corrects the son in whom he delights."*
— *King Solomon* [1]

A parent's work is to *see* the future and potential in their child, and prepare them for it through training. Many people wander through life because they have no vision for their life. They do not know who they are in relationship to God, nor do they *see* any significant purpose for their life. And so they live undisciplined regarding their identity as Abba's governing sons and daughters in the earth.

Abba Father, however, sees our destiny and our God-given significance, as well as what prevents the fullness of that significance from prospering. Our Father sees our end from our beginning and so trains us regarding our identity, potential, and purpose as His children.

Developing potential with vision for the future requires discipline. We may cringe at the word discipline, perhaps because of painful memories from abuse we experienced as a child. Some parents wrongly vent their own frustrations, or let emotions drive them when correcting their children. But such behavior is not righteous discipline, nor does it help a child to see their potential and future.

Abba Father does not discipline us like that. Ever. As we read previously, our Heavenly Father instructs earthly fathers to *not* correct a child in anger or in a way that *discourages* the child. Abusive discipline wounds the spirit and stunts the inner growth of a child. **Healthy discipline is given to empower and shape us in who we are for what we are to do.**

Remember how earlier we talked about a parent launching a child into their destiny? Like a coach with an athlete, a child needs training and proper discipline for his or her purpose to be fully realized. Divine purpose is expressed through love and service, not self-service, and for this we need training.

Abba Father disciplines us in different areas of life to make us strong in running our race. He will hone in on different areas at different times, building the muscles of faith, love, expectation, and many other areas needed for us to walk in strength as His governing children in the earth.

THE SCEPTER OF AUTHORITY

Discipline is training that includes instruction, chastening, and correction. Although the word *"discipline"* (Heb. *"muwcar"*) carries an understanding of inflicting some pain, it is *not* as hostile aggression from an angry person, but rather **as *striking* the heart of self-centeredness.**

Proverbs 22:15 says that *foolishness* is bound up in the heart of a child, but the *rod (scepter) of discipline* removes it. Did you hear that? Discipline is a scepter that trains a child for the authority that he or she is to carry. The essence of foolishness is that it is self-serving lawlessness in the heart. Foolishness releases chaos in the soul, and thus turmoil in everything around it.

Foolishness in the heart is what inspires wickedness in rulers. Wicked rulers destroy life and bring a people to ruin. Father wants righteous rulers who prosper life, not destroy it. Foolishness in the heart is an attitude that declares *self supremacy*. It is the heart of Humanism that proclaims, "*I* am god and king of my life." As "king" we enforce our own desires; as "god" we establish "truth" to be whatever we determine it to be, in order to fit our own agenda. But God says the end of that path is destruction and ruin (Prov. 14:12).

No parent wants to see their child end in ruin. How much more our Abba Father? Look at the price He has already paid to save us from our destruction.

In Scripture, a *scepter* or *rod* is a symbol of authority, correction, or a standard by which something is measured (Ezek. 40:3; Rev. 11:1). The scepter of a king represents his power of sovereign rule and judicial authority over lawlessness. Abba Father's discipline removes foolishness from our heart so that we can walk in His authority and the righteous government we were born to carry. His chastening removes lawlessness from our thinking so that we can discern wisely. He knows that carnal mindsets and fleshly reasoning hold the soul in a state of powerlessness. He understands how self-centeredness hinders our growth and true prosperity.

Discipline is key to the development of moral character. Strong moral character is key to a life of victory, integrity, and success. Character is defined as the attributes that distinguish who we are. Our character reflects the government of our *inner man*—the spirit, soul, mind, emotions, and will—and how they *manifest* through our behavior, conduct, and choices.

Right character is a critical component to true success, much more than talents or money. We have a Father who wants us to succeed in the things He created us for. Right character creates favor in relationships and right alignments. It opens doors to appointed places, empowering increase in growth and enlargement in work and ministry.

Because of this, Abba Father carefully disciplines us to bring our heart into tune with His, removing faulty thinking, and instilling His moral values in us for administering His government on earth. We are, after all, His royal children. Father's discipline re-moves the *unrighteous ruling* of our soul—the carnal and prideful mind, and the soul's naturally unruly emotions. His discipline teaches us to live in fellowship with His Spirit, and with Christ's mind.

As a child of God, our training in nobility has been appointed for us under the tutelage of the Holy Spirit. The Holy Spirit's work is to conform us to the image of the Son. The likeness of the Son is the measure for everything in our life—our character, passions, and focus. Even though God's correction of our unholy passions may be painful to our pride and flesh, He disciplines us because He loves us (Prov. 13:24). He is raising us as royal children who carry His government.

Abba Father's training is important to the prospering of our full potential in Him, a training that requires a strategic undertaking. Father has our calling, purpose and destiny in view.

CORRECTION IS AN EXPRESSION OF LOVE

Our Father's discipline is the expression of His deep love and de-light in us (Prov. 3:12). Contrary to how some view God as distant or always angry with us, the truth is that He highly esteems us. For this reason, He brings our destructive self-centeredness to the cross where we understand that *He* is God and King, and not us. He brings down the pride that grasps for exalted places as He shapes us into humble, yet mighty, sons and daughters for divine governmental positions.

We were made for government of the earth realm. The question comes in as to whether we are grasping it for selfish agendas, or receiving it from Father for His purposes. Father disciplines us to refine and mature us for rightly handling His authority for our calling as His children. **And so, the rod of discipline becomes the scepter of authority in our life and for our work**.

His discipline includes the care of the body—He cares about *every* aspect of our life. He cares how we treat our body, how we use it, what we put into it, and even our attitude towards food and drink. He knows that we can't fulfill our calling and purpose if we destroy our body through abuse or neglect.

Our Father's loving discipline not only works to root out destructive ways in us, but it *promotes courage* in us to do what is right. This results in a life of power! No flesh likes discipline in the moment, but understanding that it will produce righteousness, honor, peace, and Christ-likeness in us helps us to submit to His discipline (Heb. 12:11).

It takes trust and humility to allow someone to correct us. When we know their motive is love, and that they have our best interest in mind, correction is more readily accepted. Abba Father has our best interest in mind.

In the Old Testament, the man Job gained a deeper revelation of God's unsurpassable greatness as a result of intense discipline. Job walked through a time of incomparable suffering, but came out with a double portion. Even though he received an abundance that replaced his immense loss, the greatest blessing Job gained through it all is reflected in his powerful declaration, "I have heard of You by the hearing of the ear, but now my eyes see You" (Job 42:5).

Discipline shifted Job from knowing *about* God to *knowing* God. The trial opened his eyes to see his Creator, and it worked in him a deeper humility. Job received a divine understanding that brought priceless inward transformation.

The Father uses many ways to discipline us, including people, circumstances, and His own voice. Like a Holy Refiner of gold, He uses the fires of life to bring the impurities within us to the surface, exposing it so that it can be removed. He works diligently until He sees the reflection of Himself in the gold.

The outcome of Father's discipline is deep inward righteousness, peace, and joy, though it may not feel joyful at the time. Joy comes when we become deeply aware that we are being disciplined *because we are loved and valued.* Father doesn't want our life to be wasted through corruption, but to flourish with fullness.

TRAINED AS ROYALTY

Proverbs 22:6 says, "Train up a child in the way he should go, even when he is old he will not depart from it." The Hebrew word *"train"* (*"chanak"*) means: to make narrow. The word *"narrow"* (Grk. *"stenos"*) means: to groan, running counter to natural inclinations. It also means: to *press* as with affliction. The Father's discipline is a part of His training in our life. He is not raising us as ordinary children, but as *kings and priests* (Rev. 1:6). These two positions carry governmental authority and both require specific discipline *and* training. **The chief thing about kings and priests is that they are governmental positions of** *power and influence* **with heaven and earth.** Both are positions that release blessing for the prosperity of a people group or nation (we will read more about the blessing later).

The discipline of our Father's training presses against our *natural* inclinations. This pressing breaks away the limitations and containments of the *natural* mind that hinders us, freeing the movement of the Holy Spirit through us. In the Bible, God's people are referred to as an olive tree. An olive *press* is an instrument designed to *crush* the olive so that oil is released. Oil, in Scripture, is used for healing and anointing. Jesus went through the olive press for the healing of mankind. As Abba's children, there is an anointing of His Spirit in us that He wants released through us, and the gifts He's given us for the healing of the nations.

Our calling in God is specific, and our training is narrow and divinely strategic. **We all like the thought of having power and influence, but are we willing to go through the process that will purge out the self-centeredness that propagates corruption in places of power?** At the time of this writing, our nation is experiencing the impact of corruption in high places *and* at every level of society. Wickedness does not only operate in the hearts of many who govern as political or corporate leaders—it operates in the nature of all human flesh. Wickedness (Heb. "ra") means that which is bad, evil, corrupt, displeasing [to God], idolatrous, mischievous in purpose, unholy, unkind, and injurious. We may not see it, but Father does. Any corruption within us doesn't just hurt us, it hurts others. God didn't fashion us to hurt others, but to righteously serve others.

Corruption don't just operate in worldly systems, but, unfortunately, in many ministries as well. Even Christian ministry can be self-serving if the heart is not yielded to the Father. We can look good on the outside, but inside our thoughts and motives may be tainted with selfish ambition.

Abba Father reaches out His hand to take ours and lead us on the *narrow way* of a royal identity as His child. That way is the *way of the cross and resurrection*. The cross puts to death the old man and mind, so that the new man can be raised in *power* to live as Father's rulers and priests for the wellbeing of our families, communities, and nations.

DISCIPLINED FOR DESTINY

As Son of Man, Jesus, too, had to *learn* obedience through the things He suffered (Heb. 5:8). He chose the *narrow* way, teaching it as the *only* way to life. He also taught that the *wide* way is the way to destruction (Matt. 7:13-14). Today, He sits on the throne with Father.

Our Heavenly Brother did not come to this world riding on a blazing chariot in the radiant splendor as All Powerful God; He came in humility, as a human baby that had to grow and mature through the processes of life, just like us. He took on our form and flesh. As He grew up, most people only knew Him as the humble carpenter's son. But Jesus, knowing that He had a divine purpose to fulfill on earth, allowed the Father to discipline and train Him through suffering, rejection, years of silent labor, and the pressures of life. He allowed Father's perfect timing to order His steps. Submission to discipline matured His life as a *true* Son.

Submission to Abba Father's discipline shaped His life as a Man led of the Spirit, unhindered by the flesh, to *fulfill* His divine destiny—one that impacted the whole world, and worlds to come, forever. Father has a destiny for us to fulfill, too.

James 4:7 says we are to *submit to God and resist the devil*. The word *"submit"* (Grk. *"hypotasso"*) means: to yield to another's command or admonition; to be subject to another with obedience. The term "submit" was also a Greek military term meaning "to arrange in troop divisions in a military fashion." Submission is not about "control," but about yielding in obedience to a commander for the purpose of training and arranging us as troops!

Submission means to have a *sub mission* under a higher authority. It is not about being a subservient "doormat," but a trained ruler who knows how to war and prosper a territory. We are the army of God and each one has a calling that requires training for a divine mission. We don't choose our own mission, nor do we do our own ministry *for* God. We co-labor with Him as trained sons for ruling territory.

Submission trains us through honor to authority, cultivating in us the ability to carry authority and be sent out for the Father's purposes. We are Father's troops that He sends to establish His Kingdom in the earth. No commander sends an untrained troop into combat. It would mean their death, as well as a failed mission. Father loves us and wants us to live, fully, radiantly, victoriously. He also has a mission for us to accomplish.

Submission to Father's discipline matures us to *move with eternity with an eternal Kingdom*. We don't get those results on the *"wide"* way. In Chapter 1, *The Significance of a Father*, we learned that a father is one who brings forth those who are *animated with the same spirit as himself*. So it is with Abba Father. He trains us *so that our entire life is animated with the same Spirit as Himself.*

POLISHED AS AN ARROW

The Prophet Isaiah called himself a "polished arrow" in God's quiver (Isa. 49:2). A *"polished"* arrow is one that is shaped, cleaned, honed, and proven through testing—able to sail with speed to its designated target, and accomplish the archer's intentions. We are the Father's "arrows" prepared and placed in His quiver for His use. He sends us, not randomly, but as arrows who will hit the target of divine purpose.

Proverbs 13:18 says that *without discipline* we come to poverty and shame—that is not our Father's target! His target is that all come to the knowledge of God in Christ, in whom there is great reward. Father has a world to touch, heal, and govern through us. Will we let Him discipline, polish, and send us?

ACCEPTING CORRECTION

A child's willing acceptance of discipline reflects a core value of honor for that parent. No earthly parent feels honored when their child turns away from them to do their "own thing." It is no different with the Heavenly Father. In the Old Testament, Israel often refused to respond to God's correction and it grieved Him (Jer. 2:30). Listen to His words in Malachi 1:6-8:

"A son honors his father, and a servant his master. Then if I am a father, where is My honor? And if I am a master, where is My respect?"

Israel's dishonor toward God as a Father manifested as *refusing His correction.* It also manifested itself by the *pitiful offerings* they brought instead of giving God their best and what He required. It is *right* that God should have requirements of His children and it *honors* Him when we give Him our best. It honors Him when we embrace His correction rather than displaying an independent spirit that refuses His good discipline.

Our Father says that we have had earthly father's discipline us and we respected them—how much more should we revere divine discipline that brings us into abundant living? He commands us to not esteem His chastening lightly, or grow faint (Heb. 12:5-7, 9). He has great purposes for us—beyond what we know.

Father God disciplines *all* who belong to Him. Some accept it, some don't. But He says if we are *without* discipline, then we are illegitimate children and not true sons (Heb. 12:8-10). **Remember, the Father corrects the child in whom He *delights*** (Prov. 3:12).

DISCIPLINE AND HOLINESS

Jesus didn't just call God *"Abba Father,"* He also called Him *"Holy Father"* (John 17:11). Without discipline, God's Word says that we cannot share in God's holiness, and without holiness we cannot know His glory.

We have a divine destiny that can only be realized through the disciplines of God. His discipline is not just about *us*, but is about His love for the world *through* us. The earth that has suffered beneath the sinful government of fallen man cries out for divine government through the sons and daughters of God.

Multitudes are waiting to be healed and delivered from the curse under which they have labored. Who will be the polished arrow to be sent? Who is willing to go through the press to bring the Father's healing to those around them? Who is willing to tread serpents and join Father in His holiness?

We can have money, positions, and all that this world can give, but what does it mean if we live for ourselves while the world around us lays captive, enslaved beneath the tyranny of darkness? What life can we truly have if we are not animated with the same Spirit as our Father?

Father, discipline me in Your love. Measure me with Your golden rod and make me a pure vessel for You through which You can bring healing to the earth.

DISCIPLINED TO RULE

In closing this chapter, I want to mention another family relationship that is not the focus of this book, but is also presented in God's Word. It is our relationship to Christ as His body, His "Bride," His Church (Eph. 5). The original Greek word for *"Church"* is *"Ekklesia"* and means: a parliament, congress, a body of citizens gathered to discuss the affairs of the State.

The term "sons" is the terminology Scripture uses to describe our relationship to the Father in doing His will; a "bride" is the

154

terminology Scripture uses to describe our relationship to the Son as His body who moves as "one flesh" (one nature and work) with Him. I mention this metaphor here because being a part of this bridal company also speaks of our identity in family relationship with God as a *ruling company*, seated in heavenly places Eph. 2:6).

This "bridal company" or "Parliament" are those who are born of God's Spirit, are cherished by Him, and who have made Christ their highest treasure, forsaking every other love to be one with Him and who will reign with Him forever. They have engaged the preparation required for that ruling place—willingly submitting themselves to the Spirit's sanctifying work to be presented as a "bride" who is **pure and blameless in love** (1 Pet. 1:19; Eph. 5:27).

Satan's plan from the beginning has been to depose mankind from our intended place of authority. And so he works to defile us, so he can gloat over us (Micah 4:11-13). Our Father, however, is greater and teaches us to discern the enemy's work to keep us out of the love of God. Father says we are to be wise as serpents, yet gentle as doves (Matt. 10:16). In His training He gives us authority to tread on serpents—that python spirit that crushes life and destiny (Luke 10:19).

Our Father not only trains His sons and daughters for divine purpose, but He is also the Father of the pure in heart who love His Son and who will reign with Him for eternity.

Father, teach us to receive Your discipline and tread on the enemy, that we might rise in purity and rule as one with Your Beloved Son.

PERSONAL APPLICATION:

1. What was discipline like in your home growing up?
2. How do you respond to correction from others?
3. How do you see Father's discipline in your life? How do you respond to His discipline?
4. In what ways do you see unruliness in your soul life?

5. What area is God honing and refining in your life presently?

6. Do you see your future? What does it look like?

7. In what ways do you need discipline for that destiny?

8. List any ways that you have learned to "tread on serpents."

CHAPTER 10

OUR FATHER'S WORK

"For just as the body without the spirit is dead,
so also faith without works is dead."
—*The Apostle James* [1]

Jesus said that what voice we follow plays the role of a father in our life and determines the *works* we do—whether it be the counsel of God or the devil (John 8:41; Gal. 5:19).

At the age of twelve, Jesus sat in the temple conversing with the priests—He knew, even then, that God was His Father and that engagement with Him would shape His life and define His work. In time, that engagement and work has revolutionized the seen and unseen world, forever.

Jesus said, "My Father is working until now, and I Myself am working" (John 5:17). He also said that the Father who was *in* Him was the One who was doing the works *through* Him. If Father is working, and Jesus is working, then we, too, must work. So let's pick up our gifts and God-given calling and work!

THE WORKS OF FAITH

Abba Father has a work to do not only *in* us, but *through* us. A *"work"* (Grk. "ergon") is defined as: something with which you are occupied, an act of business, an undertaking, a deliberate engagement for the accomplishing of a thing. Jesus said, *"This is the work of God that you believe in Him whom He has sent"* (John 6:29). *"Truly, truly, I say to you, he who believes in Me, the works that I do, he will do also, and greater works than these he will do, because I go to the Father"* (John 14:12). God wants to accomplish things in the earth and it is through believing—through faith—that we join Him in His works. In fact, Father has chosen to do His works *through* us.

Our life as Abba's child begins with the work of faith—the movement of our spirit, soul, and body motivated by what we hear from God. A life of faith begins when we respond to God's dialogue with us. We hear about God's passionate love for us, and how He wants us to be reconciled to Him through Jesus. Faith enters our heart and we move; we act on that word. We enter the dialogue with God and perhaps pray something like, "I confess my sin, and surrender my life to You, Jesus, to be my Lord and Savior." Thus we began a life of listening to God and moving on what He says.

A work of faith is our engagement with the word we hear from God. Without a doubt, our whole life in Christ is one of ever unfolding engagements with God in accomplishing His purposes because the *Spirit of Faith* lives in us, and the Spirit always moves with the Father. When the Father speaks, the Spirit of faith (the Holy Spirit) rests on His words to bring forth His desires. When we agree with God's word by acting on it, divine power is released (Rom. 10:17). In other words, our movement with the Holy Spirit on what the Father says is what is called the *work of faith that accomplishes the works of God.*

When Jesus said we are to "occupy" until His return, He didn't mean to simply be busy, but to be occupied with advancing His Kingdom, the Father's Kingdom. When Jesus returned to the Father, He sent the Holy Spirit that we might continue doing greater works than He did. And this can only be done by *acting* on God's dialogue with us.

Faith itself is a spiritual substance, a spiritual energy that empowers movement on what God says. Faith listens and looks to understand God's thoughts for direction and advancement. God's words are like seed that requires faith in our heart to mix with the word to become fruitful in us and through us. God dialogues with us in many ways: as a thought, impression, picture in our spirit, a feeling, a knowing or sensing we have, a Scripture, song, dream, or word we hear in our inner man—all consistent with His Word.

God's words that are mixed with faith produce the works of faith. Works of faith display the Father's governing presence in natural circumstances. When I was a young person seeking God and desperately needing breakthrough in my life, He gave me the Scripture Jeremiah 29:13, "You will seek Me and find Me when you search for Me with all your heart." As I read that Scripture, the Spirit of faith rose up in my heart and I knew, without a doubt, that I would find Him if I did what He said—seek Him with ALL my heart.

As I moved on that word with faith, breakthrough came. It wasn't quick, it took quite some time for me to learn seeking Him "with all the heart." But meanwhile, faith kept me moving on that word. And when breakthrough came, it came with power! I sought and I found. The word had been mixed with faith.

Hebrews 11 gives us myriad examples of those who through faith touched and changed the world. A few of them include: Noah who heard God's warnings and *moved on His word* to prepare before destruction came...regardless of the mockers; Abraham who heard God speak and left everything behind to look for a city whose builder and maker was God; Sarah who bore a child in old age; and Joseph who rose from prison to a palace in a day. It tells of Moses who chose to suffer with God's people, rather than enjoy sin for a season, and at 80 years old (after 40 years of exile) became God's deliverer for His people. And the list goes on.

Jesus told His disciples to have faith in God for the impossible. He understood that the very world we live in came from the unseen, and it is from the unseen that we receive our supply for this life, and the authority we need for the works we are to do on earth (Mark 11:22; Heb. 11:3). Faith pleases the Father (Heb. 11:3).

The Apostle James charged the people of God that if faith does not have works, it is dead faith (James 2). Apathy and disengagement to what God is saying may be a result of self-will, unbelief, or a manifestation of a spirit of slumber. Whatever it is, get rid of it! The world needs men and women with works of faith that accomplish the undertakings of God for their communities and nations.

THE ACTIVITY OF PRAYER

Having engaged a new life in Christ through faith in God's words to us, another activity of faith we engage is a deeper dialogue with the Father, Son, and Holy Spirit called prayer and intercession.

Like all children, we grow and mature through communicating with parents. We mature in Christ through active dialogue with God. The disciples of Jesus understood that the power of Jesus' life and ministry was a direct result of the time He spent with the Father. They realized that to follow Jesus and engage Kingdom ministry, they would need a lot more than their own strength or ingenuity. They needed to know the Father as Jesus knew Him. And so, they approached Him and said, "Lord, teach us to pray."

And this is what Jesus prayed:

> *"Our Father who is in heaven, hallowed be Your name, Your kingdom come, Your will be done on earth as it is in heaven. Give us this day our daily bread and forgive us our debts as we forgive our debtors. And do not lead us into temptation, but deliver us from evil. For Yours is the kingdom and the power and the glory, forever. Amen." Matthew 6:9-13*

Jesus taught these new Kingdom ambassadors how to intimately relate with Abba Father through a life of intimate dialogue with Him. He began by teaching that prayer isn't religious rhetoric; it's relationship. He taught that we come to the Father as sons, not as beggars or strangers. He taught prayer as a deliberate act of worship from sons and daughters who esteem the Father's greatness, magnifying His position and authority above every earthly thing

160

or circumstance. He taught that a rich engagement with God is an expressed desire to see the Father's Kingdom be manifest on earth as it is in heaven.

Jesus' prayer demonstrated that fellowship with the Father is an act of looking to Him as the source of supply for our needs in every area, and talking to Him about it, trusting Him for it.

He showed that prayer is turning from sin and receiving Father's forgiveness regarding personal trespasses (a trespass is where we "cross the line" regarding what is right in His eyes). He showed prayer to also be forgiveness toward those who have crossed some line with us.

He taught that prayer is asking for Father's leading and the manifestation of His continual delivering power from evil that would harm us.

Jesus showed how the *movement* of prayer springs from the deep recognition that all power, glory, and honor belong to Abba Father.

Prayer has many faces, but its greatest expression is that it's an act of loving God and esteeming His heart and thoughts to be our highest priority. Love seeks communication, and when we deliberately spend time with God it shows that we not only need Him, but we love Him and believe in Him. We esteem Him through prayer.

Prayer is worship. It is an act that believes that God hears us, cares about us, and will speak to us about the situations that concern us, our families, communities, and nations. Dialoguing with Him is about seeking *His* will, not our own. Only when we get His counsel on matters can we move on what He says to us...and have faith that something divine is going to happen!

Prayer is the gateway to greater works of faith.

The disciples understood from Jesus that prayer is intimacy with God that transforms our thoughts and views, and thus impacts our works. In prayer we receive Abba's strategies and creative ideas. We see how He thinks about things, helping us to know how to respond to the issues of life, and not be cast down in hopelessness or discouragement. Prayer releases the power of God into our life, and His authority into the activities of this world to overturn the schemes of Satan. It releases angelic ministry (Ps. 103:20).

Fasting, too, is an important part of prayer. Fasting is not about trying to compel an "unwilling" God to move, but about pressing in to seek God's heart with fervor about a matter. This empowers us to act in unity with Him and with His declarations in our mouth. God is very willing...He's just waiting for someone to care more about what He has to say than the food they eat or the programs they watch. Words have assignments and we need Father's words that will effect His work in the earth.

In 2 Chronicles 29:11, God charged His sons to "not be negligent" regarding prayer—to not fail to minister to Him and "burn incense." In the Old Testament, burning incense was the place of intercession and worship in the Holy Place of the Tabernacle. Incense was taken into the Holy of Holies where God's glory dwelled and where the High Priest would commune with God.

Scripture teaches that we are kings and priests unto God. Prayer is part of our priestly activity. It is the divine work of holy sons and daughters. What's more, prayer isn't restricted to quiet times with God, but is a lifestyle. We are the temple of God and our communion with Him is 24/7, wherever we are.

I am continually aware of God. I pray when I get up, in the car, while I cook meals, as I study and work, and everywhere I go. Like with the altar of incense in the Tabernacle, communion with God is to be a perpetual, undying flame within us. In essence, the work of prayer is the flame of love that goes beyond ourselves, and our own comforts, to know God and engage with Him not only for our lives, but for the world around us.

Our Appointed Ministry

As the Father sent the Son into the world to minister His Kingdom, so are we sent by Him. We are appointed as heaven's ambassadors on earth (John 17:18; 20:21; Luke 22:29).

The word *"appointed"* means: to dispose one's affairs into the hands of another. What are the "affairs" we've been given? **Preach the kingdom, heal the sick, raise the dead, cleanse the lepers, and cast out demons.** We are appointed to **make disciples of all the nations**, baptizing them in the name of the Father, Son, and Holy Spirit, teaching them to know and do all that the Son has given us charge to do (Matt. 10:7-8; 28:18-20).

Jesus said that these things, including speaking with new tongues and having the power of life over deadly things, would be the signs that follow those who believe in His name (Mark 16:17, 18). This does *not* mean, however, that we do foolish things in order to "prove" God, as some have interpreted.

This appointment of divine affairs is another work of faith. We are commissioned as sons and daughters of God to do the same works that Jesus did. The same Holy Spirit of *power* that dwelled in Him to do the Father's work, dwells in us for the same purpose (Rom. 1:4; Acts 1:8; Rom. 15:19; 1 Cor. 5:4; 2 Tim. 1:7).

Since the Holy Spirit came at Pentecost, the ministry of the Son is now through *His body—us* (read Acts). Our work with Christ in Kingdom affairs is both in *preaching and power* to heal, deliver, and restore people with the love of God. Paul said that he himself did not minister in persuasive words of wisdom, but in *demonstration of the Spirit and power* (1 Cor. 2:4).

We cannot push back the powers of hell with merely good words and great programs. We need the *power* of the Holy Spirit to break the hold of Satan and minister restoration to people who are being held captive in darkness. We need the power of the Spirit to minister to the sick, raise the dead, and share the gospel that transforms communities from darkness to light. We need the power of the Spirit to reconcile the earth back to the designs of our Father.

Some Christians believe that God's power ceased with the New Testament days, and that He doesn't heal today. I do not see anywhere in Scripture that the Holy Spirit has stopped His ministry or has no desire to heal anymore. To not allow the Holy Spirit to move in power is to quench Him, grieve Him, and limit Him. And no one likes to be quenched, grieved or limited. Do you? I don't. And God certainly doesn't.

CARETAKERS, NOT CAPTIVES

As God's ambassadors, we are given His authority to bind devils and free those oppressed by demonic manifestations of sickness, error, witchcraft, bondage, and fear. Demonic presence also manifests through idolatry, seduction, lying, and perversion, and in some cases, blindness, deafness, and muteness. We have the authority to command demons to go. Demons are a part of this world; it's just a fact, and one we *must* deal with. We may not see them with the natural eye, but they are present and wreak terrible havoc through mankind's agreement with them. Agreement with darkness destroys lives, families, and nations. Jesus came to destroy the works of darkness. He discerned the work of the enemy and did something about it. We are to do the same.

We are no longer captives in darkness, and it's time to get up and be who we are as Abba's children of light. Our commission as God's caretakers of the earth has never changed. After man's fall in sin and prior to the cross, man simply didn't have the freedom, power, or authority for our commission—we lost them as captives in darkness through our unbelief and rebellion. Jesus, however, freed us and gave us His authority and the power of the Holy Spirit. He gives us what we need now for our work as His body.

CONNECTION

As ministers of our Father's Kingdom we are to connect with heaven *and* earth. We connect with God in prayer, hearing His voice and getting His strategies, that empowers us to also connect with people as ministers of His love. Abba wants to minister His life where there is death, light where there is darkness, and order where there is chaos. And He does it through His children.

Our Father deeply cares for people and everything that concerns what He brought forth into life. He cares about crime, health, education, and businesses. He cares about people and nations that will one day stand before Him as they move into an eternal destiny. He calls us to work with Him for their wellbeing.

OUR UNIQUE CALLING

There are actions we engage because God's Word instructs us to do so as the *general will of God* for everyone. There are also *appointed ministry* (such as what we just mentioned) that every believer is to engage. But there are also *specific works* that are *unique* to each son and daughter within God's family. In this unique work, Abba will direct each of us regarding a specific labor, location, or people group. What we do is a service or "supply" from God for helping others.

I heard a pastor once say that to be truly effective in life and ministry, we must *specialize* in the work God gives us to do. In other words, we must be intentional about His gifts in us. Ephesians 4:16 says that every believer is a unique part of Christ's body, a member that supplies what is needed to mature the body *and hold* the body together! This is so important!

Just like a physical body has individual parts each doing *unique* works, so are we to know and do our part! My thumb isn't my elbow, but what my thumb does, it does really well. It's effective! It's not confused about its place or work.

Many people I talk with don't seem to have a clear vision of what God wants them to do. They ask, "What is God's *will* for me?" But what they really want to know is God's *specific work* or unique purpose for them—something *they* are called to do in their unique way from God to help others.

While God's *appointed* work is clearly written in His Word, the *specific* work for us isn't always so clear. Why? Because it involves hearing God regarding one's unique gift-set, talents, temperament, and calling from Him. It helps us to know the particular aspects of His image in us and intentionally develop what gifts and talents He has given us. Yet, even so, our unique work can only fully be known by what Father *speaks* to us. His direction will refine the "where, when, what, and to whom" of our journey.

Our unique gifts and talents are tools for doing the will of our Father, and they can open doors where Father wants us to walk and do our appointed work. But we must also listen for the leading of the Holy Spirit as doors open before us and our "gifts make room for us." Not all doors are the ones He may want us to go through.

Remember the story of Abraham—just because Hagar was an "opportunity" to bring forth a son, it wasn't God's way for Abraham...and he knew it (Gen. 16). The conflicts that resulted from that "open door" are still prevalent in the world today. God wants us to simply listen, trust Him, and follow His leading.

Deep down everyone wants purpose, and Abba wants us to succeed in those purposes He has for us. The body of Christ longs to know the Father and do His work because the Spirit of adoption cries within us saying, *"Here I am, send me! What do You want me to do, Father?"*

As we began this chapter, we saw how faith believes God when He speaks, and that He speaks to us. Some Christians believe that God stopped speaking when the last apostle died. I'm sorry they think their Father is either mute or silent; He is not. I don't understand how they think that Jesus, the Word, is not speaking. Our fruitfulness in doing His will is intimately connected to hearing His voice. He tells us what He desires. He may speak to us in prayer, through our passions, or in a dream about the work He has for us. He may give us a burden for a specific people group or a burden may spring from something we've gone through in the past that He wants us to use to help others.

Talents, abilities, and ideas for inventions that He gives us are also given by God for the work of His Kingdom. The world is our mission field, be it in the pulpit, in the workplace, or in the home. Whatever Father has for us, He will confirm it to us.

In the 1981 British film, *Chariots of Fire* (a story based on Eric Liddell, a runner from Scotland who won the gold medal in the 1924 Summer Olympics), this statement was made: "I believe that God made me for a purpose, but He also made me fast, and when

I run, I feel His pleasure." Whether Eric Liddell really said that or not isn't important, but the truth of it remains: when we do the will of God we *feel* His pleasure...and that is also a confirmation.

There is a deep satisfaction in doing what God created us to do. When Father gives us a specific work to engage, His presence goes with us so that we are not merely laboring, but we are *co*-laboring with Him. And co-laboring with Him is from a place of rest, not striving. He doesn't strive.

I was involved in music ministry for many years, but now the Father's *unique* work for me is in speaking, training, and writing about our identity in Christ as the sons and daughters of God and as Christ's bride. When I first started writing this book some years ago (being one of my first books), God gave me a dream.

In the dream, my two children and I were sitting at school desks. There were rows of desks such as you would normally see in a classroom, except we were in the middle of a beautiful open meadow and we were the only students. In the dream, my children appeared to be about eight and nine years old or so (though in real life they were grown). The three of us were there to take a writing exam. A teacher sat before us at her desk and began timing us. My children sailed through the exam and went off to play, while I struggled. At first, I wrote a full page with ease. But then I decided it wasn't quite right. I quickly erased it all and started over. This time, the words were strained. I wrote, erased, rewrote, and erased again. When the time was up, my paper showed only a few scribbled words. I went to the teacher who graciously said I could have more time. The dream ended.

When I woke up, my first thoughts were, *No more delay! No more hindrances!* At that time in my life I had known for over thirty years that I was called to write. The thought of being a writer began to emerge when I was twelve years old, but I didn't take it seriously until I was in my late forties. Everything has its time in our lives, but it took me that long to figure out that writing the revelations that God was giving me wasn't simply *my* idea, but it was *God's* plan for my life.

God speaks in dreams, and while the dream in the meadow spoke to me on many levels, what I heard Father speak to me was that the hour is late, but I still have time to fulfill this unique work He's called me to do. He also didn't want me to be hindered by perfectionism. While I am to seek excellence, He is looking for my obedience. In my dream, my children represented childlikeness that obeys, and especially without a *fear of performance*—a fear that can hinder accomplishing what we are to do.

Stepping into the Father's work for us can be hindered by many things, including an undue focus on our own shortcomings, inadequacies, or comparing ourselves to others. Or we may be hindered simply by not recognizing the voice of God when He speaks to us about a matter. No gift is too small when we put it into God's hands. And He what He gives us, He wants multiplied.

Father wants us to be free in our work and to leave the results to Him. Look at how Jesus took a little boy's five loaves of bread and two fishes, lifted it to heaven, blessed it, and then fed thousands of people...and had leftovers! **God uses our abilities, yet He is not limited to our abilities, nor is He limited by our inabilities.** He can bring increase with whatever we give Him.

Perhaps some of you reading this book have been waiting to step into something that God has put in your heart to do, but you have been hindered by fear or perfectionism. God says, *"It's time to get up, get dressed, and put on strength. Shake off the dust of the past, and remove the chains of captivity from your neck. It's time to take your place!"* (Isa. 52:1-3). As you depend on *His* power and presence, His work through you will bear fruit that lasts (John 15:16).

THE REWARD FOR OUR LABOR

God promises that our diligent obedience *will* be rewarded. Father doesn't favor one person over another because of personality or ability; He loves and rewards each of us for our engagement with Him and faithfulness to do the work He gives us (1 Pet. 1:17). He is the *Rewarder* of those who diligently seek Him to do His will (Heb. 11:6).

God is **not unjust** so as to *not reward* us for our labor, and He promises that the *expectation* of our labor will not be cut off (Heb. 6:10; Prov. 24:14).

Promises regarding reward include:

- Reward comes to secret prayer and fasting (Matt. 6:6, 18)
- Ministering to prophets and righteous men and women makes you a partaker of their reward (Matt. 10:41)
- Ministering to the needy reaps reward (Matt. 10:42)
- Loving your enemies, doing good, and lending without return brings reward (Luke 6:35)
- Living for Christ will be rewarded with an inheritance (Col. 3:24)
- There is a *good* reward when a husband and wife labor together (Ecc. 4:9)

Our Abba Father knows that every work and field has many and varied challenges. He says, *"Do not be discouraged. Do not fear. Do not grow weary. You will reap in the appointed time"* (Gal. 6:9). Remember, Satan is a python who hates our labor and the resulting harvest that glorifies the Father. He tries to crush our spirit through discouragement, making us feel that our labor is in vain. He tries to crush the breath out of our hope and vision. But God justly rewards our obedience, so do not throw away your confidence. Continue sowing, watering, and cultivating those places where Father gives you to labor; whether with a child, in your workplace, in ministry, or wherever you go.

Abba Father wants us to sow expectantly with a vision for the harvest of our labor. He says if we sow generously, we *will* reap generously (2 Cor. 9:6). Sometimes we give up hope when we do not see the results we want, but sometimes the breakthrough is right around the corner. We must see with His perspective and not with our natural eyes. In Isaiah 41:10 God says, *"Do not fear, for I am with you; do not anxiously look about you, for I am your God. I will strengthen you, surely I will help you, surely I will uphold you with My righteous right hand."*

Be confident that He who gives the vision to sow, will also bring the rain for increase. Let your expectation be in Him alone (Ps. 62:5). If it seems the seed you've planted has failed to produce the desired harvest, remember, with God all things are possible to *him who believes* (Mark 9:23). Trust His time; He is the faithful One. With Him there is *great* reward (I Cor. 3:8; Heb. 10:35).

We must not envy others, nor compare the challenges in our labor to another's work. As Jesus said to Peter, ". . . what is it to you? You, follow Me!" (John 21:22—CJB).

OUR WORK AND MOTIVES

There are many works that we can engage in life. We can do what *Father tells* us to do, what *others ask* us to do, or what *we want* to do. We can be busy doing many things, even ministry, that has nothing to do with Father's specific work for us. Such labor will not produce the kind of fruit that Father intends through our life.

Work motivated by the approval of man, selfish ambition, or even ignorantly doing something that is good but not God-directed for us can be empty labor. I admit that I have spent precious time in the past doing some things that Father perhaps didn't specifically call me to do. In doing so, I left undone the work He *did* call me to do. It was the empty feeling I had inside one day that made me stop and listen to three questions that had been swirling inside me for some time.

Those three questions were: *What* am I doing? *Why* am I doing it? *Who* am I doing it for?

As I prayed about what I felt, I saw a picture in my spirit that brought clarity to these questions—one that changed my perception and decisions regarding some areas of ministry and service I was involved in. The picture was a vision of me standing before the Lord and behind me was a field where all my labor, time, and effort was being burned to ashes—labor that was not what Father had asked me to do. And in that moment I also saw hidden motives that were not pure, ones I didn't even know had been there.

Scripture makes it clear that those who labor for personal gain will indeed get a reward, but not the desirable kind (Jude 11). Father says we are not to work to please others or be seen of men, but in obedience to Him (Matt. 6:2-5). And He alone is to be our source of affirmation. If we look to people's affirmation, we *may* reap their temporal applause, but when the day comes to stand before the Father what shall we present Him? A fruitful harvest resulting from obedience, or a smoldering field where the wood, hay, and stubble of self-effort lay burning?

We can work really hard "for God," but what is our motive? Are we *driven* by purpose or led by the Spirit? Is our reward the pat-on-the-back and our name mentioned well and often? Or do we work in loving obedience to our Father's directives? We can do many things assuming we are pleasing God, and yet completely miss it. For example, look at Paul—before his divine encounter on the road to Damascus, he thought he was doing the will of God by killing the sons and daughters of God! Talk about missing it!

We have Kingdom affairs to attend. May we watch and work and not be sidetracked or discouraged, lest the harvest fail. Jesus promised that if we overcome and keep His works to the end, we will sit with Him in His throne, just as He sits with Father in His throne (Rev. 3:21). What an incredible reward and future we have if we do the will and work of our Father!

Father, help us to engage a deeper dialogue with You for accomplishing Your will on earth as it is in heaven. Help us to know the special work You desire us to accomplish with Jesus, and to do it with a right heart.

PERSONAL APPLICATION:

1. How is your prayer life? What does it look like?
2. How well do you connect with others? If needed, ask the Holy Spirit to show you how to improve connection; write down some goals and ways.

3. What is the unique work Father wants you to do?

4. Do you feel God's pleasure in what you do?

5. Is there anything that keeps you from stepping fully into the work God has for you?

6. *What* are you doing? *Why* are you doing it? *Who* are you doing it for?

CHAPTER 11

THE FATHER'S BLESSING

"The highest love of all finds its fulfillment
not in what it keeps, but in what it gives."
— Father Andrew [1]

One of the most influential acts a father can give to his child is the spoken blessing. Words carry power for a specific assignment and the assignment of the blessing is to bring increase. God Himself established the spoken blessing as power for prospering the success of His people.

God blessed Adam—male and female—for their work as rulers over the earth (Gen. 1:28). He blessed Noah and his sons as the beginning of a new generation after the flood. He blessed Abraham as He called him out of the familiar and into a new season of divine purpose, and to begin a new family specifically set apart for God (Gen. 12:1-3). God blessed Jacob when he returned to his place of destiny and inheritance in the Promised Land for a new season in his life. Jacob knew the power of divine blessing and wrestled with the Angel of the Lord regarding it (Gen. 32:24-32).

In the New Testament, Abba Father blessed His Son at His baptism in the Jordan River. The blessing was a needed part of Jesus' equipping for the destiny and purpose He was about to step into (Matt. 3:17). And how interesting that Jesus' first public sermon was on what? The blessing! (Matt. 5). It was the beginning of a new era in God and it had to start with the blessing. The blessing was also the last thing Jesus ministered to His disciples before returning to heaven. Through this act, Jesus released power for fruitfulness and increase for the new apostolic era and the commission to heal and disciple the nations (Luke 24:51).

God blesses us as His children so that we can increase, prosper, and be a blessing to the world, causing the world to prosper according to His beautiful designs.

GOD COMMANDS LEADERS TO BLESS

Throughout the Old Testament, God commanded Israel's kings (a king was a fathering position) to bless His people, because the blessing brought prosperity for His people to live in the fulfillment of divine purpose. God wanted His children to prosper as a nation, as one that would release His blessing to the nations.

Moses, as a "father" to the nation of Israel, blessed each of the twelve tribes (Deut. 33). And not only that, but he made sure that all Israel understood the power of both blessing and the curse before they went into the promised land (see Deut. 28:1-14). King David, as did others, also invoked God's name over God's people and blessed them as they sought the welfare and *good* of the nation (Ps. 122:7-9).

Israel's priests (a spiritual fathering position) were also commanded to bless God's people. Numbers 6:22-27 reflects one of those fatherly blessings spoken over the nation:

> *"The Lord bless you, and keep you; the Lord make His face shine on you, and be gracious to you; The Lord lift up His countenance on you, and give you peace…So they shall invoke My name on the sons of Israel, and I then will bless them."*

Did you catch that last statement? When the priest released the word of blessing, it would invoke (summon) the name of God over Israel. In doing so, God Himself would then release the power of blessing from heaven. This shows the link of agreement between an earthly agent (father) and the Heavenly Giver of good.

In this Scripture, we see God's blessing being initiated through the spoken word of His priests. We are priests unto God, and we are the body of Jesus, the High Priest (Rev. 1:6). We are Father's instruments of blessing. Men, as fathers, especially have a unique role in blessing those under their care.

EMPOWERING THE NEXT GENERATION

When Jesus called His disciples "the salt of the earth" and "the light of the world," He was calling forth their destiny through blessing that contained power for increase. The spoken blessing calls that which is not, as though it were—it calls into the seen realm what is not yet seen.

Words carry power—whether as a blessing or a curse (what dries up life). Jewish fathers and leaders have understood the power of the blessing for centuries; they practice it regularly to invoke *divine favor* upon their children, home, and work. Their words are a coveted impartation for a life of increase. God taught them the power of blessing in every area of life (Deut. 28).

When God begins something, He begins it with a blessing. God wanted a blessed family in the earth through whom He could bring forth His blessed Son who would release His blessing in the earth. So, God chose a man (Abram) and blessed him, saying that the blessing would make him a blessing to all the families of the earth (Gen. 12:2). Abraham, in turn, blessed his son, Isaac, who in turn, blessed his sons, Jacob and Esau. (17:20-21, 27). Before Jacob's death, he also blessed his sons, as well as his grandsons, Ephraim and Manasseh (Gen. 49). All who spoke blessings did so with *expectation* of its divine effect in their descendant's lives.

Fulfillment of the blessing spoken over a child was the *expected norm* as this blessed lineage walked in obedience to the LORD. Traditional Jewish fathers still speak blessings over their children and practice special impartation as their children move into young adulthood. A typical blessing includes the prayer that God would

175

make their sons as "Ephraim and Manasseh" (fruitful and forgetting the past, Gen. 48:20) and daughters as "Sarah, Rebecca, Rachel and Leah" (godly leaders, fruitful and wealthy, Ruth 4:11).

Abba Father wants us to prosper with His blessing—not merely for our sake, but to release His goodness to the world around us. The blessing of God is never meant to be self-gratifying, but to make us fruitful in ways that glorify Him and enrich others.

POSITIONED FOR BLESSING AND PROSPERITY

We may not have been blessed by a natural father, but our Abba Father *has* blessed us in Christ. This blessing means that everything that belongs to Christ, belongs to us since we are *in* Christ. We are positioned in the Son to receive heaven's wealth. We are blessed in the Blessed One of God (Matt. 21:9).

"Blessed be the God and Father of our Lord Jesus Christ, who has blessed us with every spiritual blessing in the heavenly places in Christ, just as He chose us in Him before the foundation of the world, that we would be holy and blameless before Him. In love He predestined us to adoption as sons through Jesus Christ to Himself, according to the kind intention of His will." Ephesians 1:3, 5 (Emphasis mine)

Blessings are spiritual in nature because they originate in the Spirit realm and are manifest on earth. They manifest in *every* aspect of our life including physical health, mental soundness, provision, finances, relationships, and guidance, and more. His blessing is manifest in the presence of His joy, peace, and kindness. Divine blessing works to overcome anything that is working death in our spirit, soul, or body. It operates in our spirit man to make us fruitful and increase from the inside out.

CHILDREN ARE AN INHERITANCE AND REWARD

God said that children are both an *inheritance* and *reward*— therefore they are to be blessed (Ps. 127:3). No wonder Jesus took children up into His arms and blessed them (Mark 10:16). He was empowering God's inheritance for fruitfulness and increase!

Just as an earthly parent's greatest joy is to see their children blessed and successful, so it is with our Father in heaven. Having *many* royal sons and daughters whose lives are rich in fruitfulness and authority makes a *full inheritance* and *rich reward* for Him.

In light of what Father teaches us, all parents should bless their children regularly with peace, wisdom, a prayer for divine guidance, and protection from evil. Leaders should bless those under their leadership. This is the Father's heart from generation to generation. **People should be blessed into their destiny.** As a child is prosperous, their prosperity becomes a *blessing* to the parents and leaders who have trained them.

A father's blessing is the act of a father seeing the destiny of a child and calling it out. A father's blessing awakens the callings and gifts within his child.

Unfortunately, not all fathers—natural or spiritual—understand the power of the blessing, or worse, what their curse words produce in those under their care and leadership. I have seen what happens in lives who have experienced a parent's cursing them. I have experienced firsthand the shutdown that results from a *spiritual* leader's curse words over a congregation.

Even though my earthly father was not taught from his father to impart a father's blessing, I did experience his love and healthy communication. I have also experienced the healing impartation and blessing from spiritual fathers that God has placed in my life. I would chance to say that many in Western culture have never received a father's blessing. But the truth is, we were created to prosper through blessing and Abba has given us His blessing in Christ. I believe the restoration of the Father's blessing is one of the keys to healing our families and our nation.

EXPERIENCING THE BLESSING

For many years, my husband and I enjoyed the privilege of being in a church where not only did the leadership bless the people, but the people were taught to bless one another. Imagine that— Christians who bless one another!

In 1999, when the Lord led our family to be a part of a church called River of Glory in Plano, Texas, we were in a time of healing from some significant abuse that had taken place in a previous church. It was the first time I had seen the spoken blessing demonstrated…and I have been in church all my life! The pastor would often take time to lay hands on the people and impart blessing. The people, too, would take time to *bless one another* (not just greet one another) as a regular part of church services. And not only that, but we were taught to minister the blessing of God wherever we went.

That experience of imparted blessing not only brought healing to our lives, but I saw how it awakened and ignited the gifts and calling of God in my life. This is what the blessing does.

Abuse and cursing shuts people down and negatively impacts gifts and calling. The blessing brings increase and God wants His people blessed. I have seen *countless* lives restored and become fruitful through the power of love and a spoken blessing.

The following are some general facts about the blessing:

- It is verbal—not merely a wish or desire (Gen. 1:28)
- It is given by Father God to His children (Gen. 1:28; Matt. 25:34; Ps. 3:8)
- It is released where there is unity of God's children (Ps. 133:3)
- It manifests through increase and authority (Mark 8:7; Matt. 24:46)
- It is evidenced in covenant with God (Isa. 61:9; Isa. 44:3)
- It is God's manifest favor upon His people (Ezek. 34:26)
- It releases joy (Ps. 21:6)
- It is found in the blood of Christ (1 Cor. 10:16)
- It exalts a city (Prov. 11:11)
- It makes one rich and He adds no sorrow to it (Prov. 10:22)
- It cannot be revoked once given (Gen. 27:33; Num. 23:20)
- It is released through obedience so that we are (Deut. 28:1-14):

- ○ Overtaken by the blessing of God
- ○ Blessed wherever we go
- ○ Blessed with children who are blessed
- ○ Blessed with provision
- ○ Abundantly prosperous
- ○ Blessed as the head and not the tail
- ○ Blessed with favor to enter places where others cannot go
- ○ Renowned as a people set apart for God
- ○ Blessed with victory when enemies rise against us
- ○ Blessed with an open storehouse in heaven
- ○ Blessed with rain that brings increase
- ○ Blessed in the work of our hand
- ○ Blessed as givers, not borrowers

The spoken blessing is given with divine purpose:

- • To make us a blessing (Gen. 12:2; 22:17-18)
- • To fulfill our commission with increase and authority (Gen. 1:27-28; 35:11-12; Matt. 14:19)
- • For the manifestation of God's glory (Lev. 9:22-24)
- • To call out prophetic destiny (Gen. 24:60; 27:27-29; Deut. 33)
- • To change our nature and make us fruitful (Gen. 35:9-12)

Selah! Take a moment to soak in these powerful truths about the blessing of God for our lives. Abba Father desires us to walk in His blessing, not for self-centered gain, but to be a blessing as the manifest sons and daughters of God that this world is waiting to see—a blessed family that is rich in Christ.

THE EFFECTUAL BLESSING

The recipient of the blessing also has responsibility for the blessing to be *effectual*. As children, we have our part in presenting our life as a place where God's blessing can *rest* with effectiveness. We cannot practice a life of sin and rebellion against God *and* expect to increase and prosper in Christ for our life and calling.

We saw how Jacob desired his father's blessing, but divine blessing requires humility. As Jacob wrestled with the Angel of the Lord, God did two things: He blessed Jacob, and yet put Jacob's thigh out of place, causing him to limp the rest of his days. That encounter brought manifest change to Jacob's walk. He was never the same (Gen. 32). That moment of blessing also caused this man of God to walk more humbly, more dependent, on the One who had blessed him.

We want God's blessing, but are we willing for His presence to touch us and change how we walk? Are we willing to walk humbly with God in a blessed life? Blessing with humility makes our life a blessing to others. Blessing without humility can make us arrogant and destructive. Jesus, the **Blessed One**, said, *"Learn of Me; for I am meek and lowly in heart"* (Matt. 11:29).

Actions that make the blessing effectual in our lives include:

> ➤ Faith in God's Word (Gal. 3:9; Luke 1:45)
> ➤ Believing *before* seeing (John 20:29)
> ➤ The fear of the Lord (Ps. 112:1; 128:1, 4)
> ➤ Delighting in, and meditating on, God's Word (Ps. 1:1-3)
> ➤ Trusting God and making Him our source (Ps. 2:12; 34:8; 84:5, 12)
> ➤ Receiving God's forgiveness (Ps. 32:1; Rom. 4:7, 8)
> ➤ Practicing righteousness (Ps. 106:3; 112:2)
> ➤ Refusing offense (Luke 7:23)
> ➤ Steadfastness with God (Ps. 40:4)
> ➤ Moral purity and purity of heart (Ps. 24:3-5; 119:1)
> ➤ Sharing with the poor, being generous (Ps. 41:1; Prov. 11:25; 22:9)
> ➤ Ministering to the poor and handicapped (Luke 14:12-14)
> ➤ Honoring God with your *firstfruits* (Ezek. 44:30)
> ➤ Abiding in God's presence (Ps. 65:4; 84:4)
> ➤ Continual praise and thanksgiving (Ps. 84:4)

➤ Allowing God to discipline us and instruct us from His Word (Ps. 94:12)

➤ Seeking God with the whole heart (Ps. 119:2)

➤ Following the ways of wisdom (Prov. 8:32-33)

➤ Waiting on God's timing to bring things about (Prov. 20:21)

➤ Faithful stewardship (Luke 12:43; Prov. 28:20)

➤ Believing and declaring what God says (Matt. 16:17)

➤ Persevering under trial (James 1:12)

➤ Believing the prophecy of the book of Revelation (Rev. 1:3)

➤ Hearing and obeying God (Deut. 29:9; Exod. 39:43; 1 Chron. 22:13; Luke 11:28)

➤ Having our garments washed (Rev. 22:14)

➤ Seeking the peace of Jerusalem (Ps. 122:6)

THE BLESSING DUE TO OUR FATHER

Our Father *delights* to prosper and bless us. And not only that, He *teaches* us to prosper (Deut. 28:63; Gen. 39:3) However, it is important to know *all* of what Father says about our prosperity and blessing. **God's Word tells us that the first *portion* of increase and fruitfulness *belongs* to God, that being, the tithe** (Lev. 27:30). In Scripture, this included income as well as produce, livestock, and offspring as the law of *firstfruits* (Exod. 34:26).

Psalm 115:18 says, *"But as for us, we will bless the Lord from this time forth and forever..."* **Our Father has blessed us, and we in turn bless Him.** He is worthy to receive the honor of all that we have because of Him. To express this honor, we not only worship Him with our heart, words, songs, prayer, and abilities, but with our finances and the fruit of our labor in tithes and offerings.

The ***tithe*** is the first portion of our income that He says *belongs* to Him. We also demonstrate our thankfulness to Him with ***offerings*** (what is given *after* the tithe). Gratitude that blesses our Father with our finances is *right conduct* as His children. He doesn't need our money, but giving it to advance His purposes on earth is a way of also showing our trust in Him as our source and provider. Withholding the financial blessing dishonors Him.

BLESSED TO BE A BLESSING

During the U.S. presidential election of 2008, a comment was made about "sharing the wealth." While the U.S. was not founded on laws that mandate "sharing" (such as socialism), caring for the poor and the sick *is* a divine charge given to the Church.

Helping others is a *freewill* offering. This is different than "enforced sharing," or better known as "entitlements." A freewill offering is part of blessing others simply because we love them, and it pleases Abba Father.

Abba Father's own nature is to be generous. He is a giving God who gives freely and liberally. As His children, we too are to be generous — we have our Father's nature. As such, He tells us not to covet what others have, but to be content with what we've been given. There will always be those who have more and those who have less. Life is not about having stuff. However, Jesus also said the poor will always be with us and there are some basic "stuff" they need! We are responsible to help them.

Covetousness and greed are powers at work in every sphere of life, and no doubt in every nation — from government to corporate offices to personal choices. The question that only we can answer individually, through prayer, is if the blessing we've been given is serving to bless our own comfort at the neglect of ministering to those in need.

Generosity and caring for the poor and needy can only happen as our hearts are free from greed, so that the blessing Father gives us can be used as He desires. The God whose heavenly streets are made of gold doesn't *need* our money, but He does *want* our heart. Food and clothing for those in need requires finances; God needs hearts that are willing to cheerfully share their blessing.

Jesus instructed His disciples both to *take money* and *not take money* with them as they travelled and ministered (Luke 22:35-36).

He taught both—while they learned their sufficiency in all things was from God (not from how much they had in their coin purse), they were to also understand that finances *were* needed to bless others. We must learn this, too.

The disciples had already witnessed the demise of one comrade whose heart was controlled by covetousness, Judas (John 12:6). Watch what God allows to be put into your hand—money is power and can be a blessing or a downfall. 1 Timothy 6:10 says, the *love of money* is the root of all evil. Money is not evil. Covetousness is.

In the New Testament, we see different ways of how people related to money. In the early Church, converts would freely bring money to the apostles for them to **distribute** to the poor and those in need. However, one couple who *lied* about their financial giving was struck dead—not by the apostles, but by God Himself (Acts 4:35; 5). Their lying and selfish motives were a blatant contrast to a crucified life in Christ—one they apparently were touting. God says He will not be mocked.

One of the Kingdom parables told by Jesus was about a lord who entrusted money to his servants. He wanted them to increase what he gave them for prospering his household. One servant buried his money instead of seeking wisdom in how to multiply it. Later, he was punished as an unfaithful servant (Matt. 25).

God's Word has a lot to say about finances, and how multiplying what we've been given is an important issue with our Father. The days we are living in requires a shift in how we relate to God, people, our gifts, and our finances. Abba Father wants to teach us a new paradigm of how to increase through His wisdom and counsel for the benefit of His household. If we are to increase, our heart must be free from greed.

Doug Hagedorn of *Financial Foundations Builders* reports that we are more prosperous as a nation, and as individuals, than ever before, yet, we give less, are more counseled, more divorced, and more in debt than any previous generation. Statistics show that only a meager 5% of adult Americans tithe and that charitable giving is a mere 2.6%. People are paying more in yearly credit interest than in yearly giving.[2]

As Abba Father's children, our *view* of money is to operate with heaven's perspectives, not from earthly mindsets. While Father wants us to give, He also doesn't want us to live in debt. Debt is *financial captivity* to another. We are called to walk in liberty in every area. Like Jacob, our new birth in Christ should reflect a walk of humility with God that moves in agreement with Him, including with our finances.

God wants to open the store house of heaven to us, but He also wants us to be a *conduit*, not a vacuum, of His blessings.

THINGS THAT HINDER THE BLESSING

While the Father has given us all blessings in Christ, it is important for us to understand that there are things that can hinder the blessings' full operation in our lives. Ungodly attitudes and actions we engage can hinder the flow of divine power in us, as well as make place in our life for curses to operate (Prov. 26:2). A curse causes dryness, barrenness, and hindered productivity in our lives, which is the opposite of blessing.

Things that hinder the power of blessing in our lives:
- Practiced disobedience to God (Deut. 28:15-45)
- Adultery (Prov. 22:14)
- Turning away from God (Heb. 6:4-8)
- Living by the works of the law as our *means* of salvation (Gal. 3:10, 13)
- Not listening to God and not honoring Him (Mal. 2:2)
- Robbing God of tithes and offerings (Mal. 3:8-9)
- Putting trust in man and the flesh over God (Jer. 17:5)
- Negligence in doing Father's will (Jer. 48:10)
- Cowardice in battle (Jer. 48:10)
- Unbelief (Matt. 13:58; Heb. 3:19)

SOWING AND REAPING

The very laws of nature demonstrate that we reap what we sow. Scripture teaches that in sowing to righteousness there is great reward. Some blessings are released when certain actions are taken. Look at the following:

REQUIREMENT — FULFILLMENT

We obey the Lord — we are overtaken by blessing (Deut. 28:1-13)

We believe God — He performs His Word in us (Luke 1:45)

We are poor in Spirit — the kingdom of heaven is ours (Matt. 5:3, 5)

We mourn — We receive comfort (Matt. 5:4)

We are meek — We inherit the earth (Matt. 5:5)

We hunger and thirst for righteousness — We are satisfied (Matt. 5:6)

We show mercy — We obtain mercy (Matt. 5:7)

We are pure in heart — We will see God (Matt. 5:8)

We are a peacemaker — We are known as God's son (Matt. 5:9)

We are persecuted for righteousness — We inherit the kingdom (Matt. 5:10, 11)

We watch for His return — We sit and dine with Jesus (Luke 12:37)

We bless the poor and needy — We receive eternal reward (Luke 14:14)

We persevere under trial — We receive the crown of life (James 1:12)

Our robes are washed — We eat from the tree of life (Rev. 22:14)

PROSPERING THROUGH GOD'S PRESENCE

In Scripture, God's presence is associated with provision and prosperity. These have always been a part of God's manifest presence with His covenant people. They are a testimony of His goodness and *who* He is to those who love Him (Ps. 35:27).

All through the Old Testament, as God's covenant people walked with Him they were prosperous *and* victorious against their enemies. Even in times of famine, God would designate places for His people to prosper. As they obeyed His voice, they increased (Gen. 26:1-12).

As long as the heart of God's people was turned toward Him and worshipped Him, keeping themselves from idols, His blessing continued with them. Times of judgment came on them because of continued idol worship. It was their hardened attitude of waywardness that hindered the flow of God's blessings. Some Christians seek prosperity for personal gain while others shun *any* thought of prosperity. Again, Father delights in our prosperity, but not for selfish reasons. Remember too, true prosperity is not about money, but about being rich in our spirit that causes us to prosper in our soul, gifts, and activities, including finances.

God's Word promises that the one who **trusts God** *will* prosper (Prov. 28:25). A life rooted in loving **dependence on God** prospers (Judg. 17:13). **God's presence** causes us to prosper as triumphant against enemy rule in our life (2 Kings 18:7). **Seeking God and doing His will** (with all our heart) causes us to prosper (2 Chron. 31:21). God promises that the one who **fears Him** will be taught of Him, and his *soul* will *abide* in prosperity (Ps. 25:13; 3 John 1:2).

God leads His children not only *out* of bondage, but *into* inheritance, promises, and prosperity (Ps. 68:6). He also says, however, that it is the *humble* and the *righteous* who prosper with His blessings and obtain promises (Ps. 37:11; Prov. 13:21).

Another part of our prosperity is the blessing that our enemy's weapons formed against us will **not** prosper; and that we have His authority to condemn every tongue that accuses us. This is our heritage as the children of God (Isa. 54:17).

BLESSING ONE ANOTHER

James 3:9-10 says we are to bless others and *not* curse them, including those who curse, mistreat, and persecute us (Luke 6:28;

Rom. 12:14). We all go through times when we may feel mistreated, misunderstood, misrepresented, or misjudged. It is part of life on earth. But our Father says we are not to return evil for evil, or insult for insult (1 Pet. 3:9). Rather, we are to pray for those who hurt us, and bless them. We can pray for their wisdom, a tender heart, divine revelation, the work of grace in their life, and even deliverance from the schemes of the enemy in their soul.

Christians should never curse or verbally abuse any other human being, and I will add, including political leaders with whom we adamantly disagree. Instead, we are to pray for them as people (and rebuke spirits). When we are merciful toward others, we reap mercy in our own life: *"Blessed are the merciful, for they shall receive mercy"* (Matt. 5:7).

Using our mouth to bless in a way that pleases our Father also includes the practice of healthy *"self-talk"*—whether out loud or in our mind. However, saying things like: *I'm stupid, I hate myself, I'm a misfit, I'll never make it, no one loves me, I'm a failure,* or any other negative declaration against ourselves is self-cursing and is from the pit of hell. As a young person, I spoke such words, but Abba Father has taught me to love who I am and use my mouth for *His* words, and not for cursing—others or myself!

Our mouth was given to us to be a tool in the hand of God, not a tool for the assignments of the world, the flesh, or the devil! If you need to repent of self-cursing, then please take a moment and do so now. Here is a prayer of agreement with God about yourself:

Father, You love me so much. You created me in Your own image. I repent of any words I have spoken that have demeaned, despised, dishonored, or rejected who I am. I come into agreement with You and how You see me. I bind all spirits of self-hatred or unforgiveness toward myself, and I loose them from me now. I ask You, Holy Spirit, to go to the root of every lie I have believed about myself, and show me the truth. I break agreement now with every unrighteous way of thinking. Father, thank You that I am blessed of You. I decree that I am accepted fully and completely in the Son, and I am affirmed and loved deeply by You, Abba Fa-

ther. *You have made me beautiful and awesome as an expression of Your likeness. I have everything I need in Christ. In Jesus' name, Amen.*

IMPARTATION OF BLESSING

You may have never received a spoken blessing from an earthly parent, but Abba Father calls you *blessed*. He sees your future, and He *will* bring about His good purposes in your life. Look at the life of David—he wasn't even recognized by his own father when the Prophet Samuel came to anoint him to be king of Israel (1 Sam. 16). But God recognized him. Abba recognizes you, too. You are your Abba's treasured child.

> **"'For I know the plans that I have for you', declares the LORD,**
> **'plans for welfare and not for calamity**
> **to give you a future and a hope.'"**
> **- Jeremiah 29:11**

And now, I would like to speak a blessing over you from Father:

The Lord bless you, and keep you and make His face to shine on you, be gracious to you, and give you peace. May the Lord bless you with strength and hope, and may you prosper in your fullest potential for which you were created. May you be rooted and grounded in Abba's love and grow strong and confident in all that He has for you. May you be abundantly fruitful in the work you've been called to do, and favored in the relationships He has for you. May you hear His voice clearly and succeed as a heavenly ambassador for earth's good. May you dream the dreams of God and know mysteries and strategies as you become all that God has designed you to be. May the Father of glory bless you with the Spirit of wisdom and revelation in the intimate knowledge of Jesus, and may you know the plans of God regarding you. May your horizons each day be filled with fresh vision as the sun of His great power illumines you and shines over you. May your days be many and your life rich in the purposes for which you were fashioned for such a time as this.

Heavenly Father, thank You for Your blessing over us that causes us to prosper and succeed in the things You have for us as Your sons and daughters. We love You, and we bless You in return.

PERSONAL APPLICATION:

1. In what ways do you see God's blessing in your life?
2. In what ways are you blessing others?
3. How are you blessing the Father with what He's given you? How about with your finances?
4. What is your self-talk like—full of blessing or cursing?
5. Do you know of anything in your life that is hindering the blessing from operating?

CHAPTER 12

For

LOVE *of the* FATHER

"But that the world may know that I love the Father,
and as the Father gave Me commandment, so I do..."
— Jesus [1]

What we have learned brings us to the understanding that the Father's love is where it all begins and ends. A child's very existence is the fruit of a father's love. We are the fruit of Abba Father's love who sent the Son and the Spirit that we might know Him.

We were created by God, we belong to Him, and one day we will see Him fully, *face to face*. Meanwhile, His Spirit in us journeys us into our divine purpose as His presence shapes our life for His good plans to release heaven on earth.

The work of Christ opened the way for us to know God's fathering. Jesus walked on earth with a heavenly mission to destroy everything that separates us from Abba's love. The fall of mankind was a fall *away* from the love of God, but our loving Brother returns us to a life immersed in God's love. That fiery love is the spring from which we are fashioned to freely and fully flourish in divine purpose. We can now live—not for self, and not alone—but in the love of God.

In Christ, we have a new framework—a life in fellowship with the Father, Son, and Holy Spirit. In this intimate fellowship we are given a mission to love that is expressed through service, just like Jesus' love was expressed through service. We serve our homes, communities and the nation where He has placed us with the understanding that we are here for such a time as this.

The Apostle Paul tells us that *love is not self-seeking*, but seeks to honor the Father and the wellbeing of others. At the celebration of the last supper, Jesus prayed that just as Father had loved Him, we would know that *same love* and a love for one another (John 17:26; John 15:9-12).

When God pulled my life out of the dark pit in which I was trapped as a young person, there was one resounding word I heard calling to me from the Light. That word was love. It is still the word that calls me out of every shadow that remains. **We love, because we are loved** (1 John 4:19).

Life isn't about things or positions. It isn't about pleasures or powers. Life isn't about what we get, but what we give. And what Father has for us to give is laced with *eternity* as we minister the heartbeat of eternal life in Christ. Even practical things we give to others like food, shelter, and a helping hand is laced with eternity when given by a heart of love. As we serve and decree the blessing of God into our spheres of influence lives are changed.

Our new framework of community with Abba Father, Jesus, and Holy Spirit infuses eternity into everything we do; business becomes a place for Father's presence to be known, and talents become a tool for the Holy Spirit to flow through; all of life becomes a venue through which Jesus can minister the Father's Kingdom through us to a broken world.

Jesus loved the Father more than His own life—this is the same image into which we are being transformed...eyes of pure love, feet that burn with judgment against injustice, and words that wields truth in love to sever the lies that hold people captive.

LOVE MADE PERFECT

1 John 2:5 says that God's love is perfected in us by doing what He says in His Word, by revering the Father's Voice as the counsel we embrace, the wisdom we seek, and the knowledge we act on. The spirit of the world does not revere Father's Voice, but rather it opposes Him. But the sons and daughters of God are *"animated by the same Spirit"* by which Jesus is animated—a Spirit of being one with the Father.

The love of self made us *powerless*, but we are not powerless anymore, for God's love has *empowered* us for a divine plan and destiny. As brothers and sisters in Christ, our love for each other is the evidence by which the world sees our faith in Jesus (John 13:35). As children of our Father, we love the world as He loves it, but we don't love the *spirit of the world* or its ways. To do so is evidence that the love of the Father is not in us.

The Apostle James said that *friendship* with the world—the lust of the flesh, lust of the eyes, and pride—are not from Abba Father; these make us hostile toward God. They are part of a world that is passing away, but the one who does God's will lives forever (James 4:4; 1 John 2:15-17).

I'm grateful that Jesus' work on the cross destroyed the power of sin that drove me away from the heart and will of God. Jesus writes on my heart the *law* of God—the *law of love* that obeys the Father's will and engages with Him in our Abba's work.

The love of God is made perfect in us by the Spirit, and as we abide in the teachings of Jesus Christ, bringing us more and more into deeper intimacy with the Father and Son (2 John 1:9).

THE MIND OF THE SON

In the book of Revelation, we read of the Apostle John's heavenly vision of the end-times. There he sees Jesus, as well as the beast, the dragon, and the false prophet. He sees how the anti-Christ operates and wars against God's people. He sees the destruction that would ravage the earth because of the anti-Christ spirit—a spirit that will operate in the leaders of many nations and in the people as well.

John identified the anti-Christ spirit as the rejection of Jesus Christ as Lord and Savior...and therefore a rejection of the Father who sent Him. This is what it means, John said, to *deny* the Father and the Son (1 John 2:22, 23). This is the *spirit of antichrist* at work.

John also saw, however, 144,000 with the *Father's name written in their foreheads*. We talk about the mark of the beast, but Father's children also have a mark on their forehead; it is the name of Divine Love. The forehead symbolizes mindsets. Jesus had many marks—those left by the crown of thorns He wore for us, and those left by the nails and the sword that pierced His side. But these all represented the greatest one of all—the mark etched on His mind of the greatness and love of His Father.

We have been given the mind of Christ as sons and daughters who love our Heavenly Father. Our mind does not belong to the world, the flesh, or the devil, it is set apart for the Father.

FOR THE LOVE OF OUR FATHER

There is a day coming when the world will fear, and chaos will abound on every side as the nations rise against God and His anointed. There will be a great apostasy—a falling away from the love of God by many—but there will also be a great host of the redeemed rising in the love of the Father. This great host is now rising up with a single eye focused on One—Jesus, the Redeemer who brings us into the depths of Abba Father's love.

These are the host who do the greater works of Christ, doing exploits because they know their God. They move as a *united troop* doing the Father's will on earth as it is in Heaven. These are the sons and daughters of God. These are those who understand that we have not been left fatherless in this world.

It isn't enough to know that God is *a* Father, but that He is *our* Father—Jesus' Father, *your* Father, and mine. Our days are meant to be lived in divine purpose by being fathered by God as *our* Dad, our Holy "Papa."

1 Peter 1:17 says that if we claim God as our Father, then we must be careful to revere and honor Him as such *"during our stay on earth."* In doing so, we understand that we will receive our reward accordingly. Just as earthly fathers are rewarded for their labor by children who honor them and heed their words, so God is rewarded by the honor we give Him through a life that glorifies Him. **May we never lose sight of the great privilege we have of being called the children of the Living God** (1 John 3:1).

I pray that after reading these pages, you have encountered a deeper place of knowing the Father, Son, and Holy Spirit *who see your future* and who is working intimately with you for a full destiny in divine purpose. May your life be rooted and grounded in Christ's love, and may you minister eternity wherever you go through the presence of the Holy Spirit. May you know the height and depth, the width and breadth of God's love, doing all things for the love of the Father.

Abba Father loves you.

Abba, thank You for the greatness of Your love for us. May we show the world our love for You in return.

PERSONAL APPLICATION:

1. What motivates your choices and decisions?
2. What does loving and serving others look like to you?
3. Have you experienced times when acts of love made you sense the power and presence of God?
4. How do you see yourself "moving as a troop" with the body of Christ?
5. What is most often at the helm of your thoughts?
6. Do you know how much Abba Father loves you?

Knowing God's Name

There are more than seven hundred names of God in Scripture. A name speaks of one's nature and character. To know God's name is to know His nature. Here are just a few of God's names.

I Am—the Self Existing One (Exod. 3:14)

Jehovah—the One who is (Gen. 2:7)

Jehovah-Jireh—God who provides (Gen. 22:14; Phil. 4:19)

Jehovah-Rapha—God who heals (Exod. 15:26)

Jehovah-Nissi—God is my banner (Exod. 17:15; 2 Chron. 20:17)

Jehovah-M'kaddesh—God who sanctifies and sets me apart (Lev. 20:7)

Jehovah-Shalom—God of peace (Judg. 6:24; Isa. 26:3)

Jehovah-Tsidkenu—God our righteousness (Jer. 23:5-6; Gal. 3:6)

Jehovah-Rohi—God my Shepherd (Ps. 23:1)

Jehovah-Shammah—God who is there (Eze. 48:35; Ps. 139:7-8)

Elroi—God who sees me (Gen. 16:13)

Almighty (Gen. 17:1)

Creator of Heaven and Former of Earth (Isa. 45:18)

Creator of Israel (Isa. 43:15)

Defender (Ps. 68:5)

Deliverer (2 Sam. 22:17-20)

Eternal God (Deut. 33:27)

Ever-Present Help (Ps. 46:1; 33:20)

Faithful Creator (1 Peter 4:19)

Father of Compassion (2 Cor. 1:3)

Father of Glory (Eph. 1:17)

Forgiving God (Neh. 9:17; Ps. 99:8)

Former of Mountains & Creator of Wind (Amos 4:13)

God my Husband (Isa. 54:5)

God my Stronghold (Ps. 18:1-3)

God of all Comfort (2 Cor. 1:3)

God of all Grace (1 Pet. 5:10)

God of Hope (Rom. 15:13)

God of Hosts (Amos 4:13)

God of Peace (Isa. 9:6; Acts 5:30)

God of Truth (Ps. 31:5; Isa. 65:16)

God of the Living (Luke 20:38)

God who avenges (Ps. 94:1)

Great & Powerful God (Neh. 1:5)

Holy One (Isa. 43:15; Josh. 24:19)

Incorruptible God (Rom. 1:23)

Judge (Gen. 18:25)

Living God (Josh. 3:10; Isa. 37:17)

Loving God (John 3:16)

Mighty Warrior (Jer. 20:11)

Miracle working God (Ps. 77:14)

My Shield (2 Sam. 22:3)

Redeemer (Isa. 49:7)

Rescuer (Ps. 140:1)

Refiner (Ps. 66:10)

Refuge in Times of Trouble (Ps. 9:9)

The Only Wise God (Rom. 16:27)

EndNotes

Introduction

1. Isaiah 64:8.

2. Abba: http://en.wikipedia.org/wiki/Ab_(Semitic), (February 16, 2015).

3. What does "Abba" mean:
http://www.christianleadershipcenter.org/otws12.htm;
http://www.thegospelcoalition.org/article/factchecker-does-abba-mean-daddy, (February 16, 2015).

Chapter 1

1. George Herbert, "Father Quotes,"
http://www.quotery.com/quotes/one-father-is-more-than-a-hundred-schoolmasters/, (February 16, 2015).

2.Father: Romans 6:4,
http://www.blueletterbible.org/Bible.cfm?b=Rom&c=6&t=KJV&p=0#s=t_c
onc_1052004, (February 29, 2008).

3.Father: Romans 6:4,
http://www.blueletterbible.org/Bible.cfm?b=Rom&c=6&t=KJV&p=0#s=t_c
onc_1052004, (February 29, 2008).

4. Fred H. Wright, *Manners and Customs of Bible Lands,* Chicago:
Moody Press, 1953, pp. 103-104.

5. Ibid.

Chapter 2

1.Jim Valvano, "Father Quotes,"
http://www.brainyquote.com/quotes/quotes/j/jimvalvano358465.html#S7
473YG2o89EqHAc.99, (February 16, 2015).

2. Certain concepts of family roles are taken from *Sozo* ministry, Bethel
Church, Redding, California. July, 2008.

Chapter 3

1. Princess Diana, "Father Quotes," http://www.brainyquote.com/quotes/topics/topic_family.htm, (February 16, 2015).

2. Facts on fatherless kids: www.dads4kids.com/facts on fatherless kids, and www.fathersunite.org, (February 16, 2105).

3. Fatherless statistics: http://fatherhoodfactor.com/us-fatherless-statistics/, (February 17, 2015).

4. Fatherlessness in Canada: www.canadiancrc.com, (July 1, 2008).

5. Effects of Fatherlessness: Hope for Tomorrow.net, http://www.hopefortomorrow.net/Did%20You%20Know.php, (February 17, 2015).
6. Fatherlessness: http://www.fathersunite.org/statistics_on_fatherlessnes.html, (February 16, 2015).

Chapter 4

1. Psalm 27:10
2. Gary Chapman, "The Five Love Languages of Teenagers," Chicago: Northfield Publishing, 2000.

Chapter 5

1. Romans 8:15.
2. Walter A. Elwell, *Baker Theological Dictionary of the Bible,* "Fatherhood of God," Grand Rapids Michigan: Baker Books, 1996, p. 247.

3. See also Rom. 8:17; Eph. 3:6; Titus 3:7.

Chapter 6

1. Beau Bridges, "Father Quotes," http://www.brainyquote.com/search_results.html?q=beau+bridges, (February, 16, 2015).

2. Tender Plant, Isaiah 53:2, http://www.blueletterbible.org/Bible.cfm?b=Isa&c=53&t=KJV&p=0#s=t_conc_732002, (February 16, 2015).

3. E. W. Bullinger, The Witness of the Stars, Kregal Classics; Reprint Edition, August, 2003.

Chapter 7

1. Johann Friedrich Von Schiller, "Father Quotes,"
http://www.quotery.com/quotes/it-is-not-flesh-and-blood-but-the-heart-which/, (February 16, 2015).

2. Matt Brumm and Jacqueline Foster, "Brain Constantly Searches for Patterns," The Chronicle, posted April 23, 2002,
http://www.dukechronicle.com/articles/2002/04/24/brain-constantly-searches-patterns#.VOJQiikpmVg, (February 16, 2015).

3. Tero International, Inc., "The Brain's Search for Patterns,"
http://www.tero.com/patterns.html, (November 11, 2014).

Chapter 8

1.Ken Venturi, "Father Quotes,"
http://www.brainyquote.com/quotes/quotes/k/kenventuri539772.html, (February 16, 2015).

Chapter 9

1. Proverbs 3:11.

Chapter 10

1. James 2:26.

Chapter 11

1. Father Andrew, "Father Quotes," http://www.quotes.net/quote/10067, (February 16, 2015).

2.Brian Kluth, "Financial and Giving Trends & Statistics: 1950s-2000s," http://www.kluth.org/church/Financialtrends1950-2000.htm, (November 4, 2008). Site references Ease the Squeeze by Doug Hagedorn.

Chapter 12

1. John 14:31

OTHER BOOKS
BY J. NICOLE WILLIAMSON

The Empowered Woman
Restoring Women to their True Identity

The Esther Mandate
The War for America's Destiny

Heaven's Secret of Success
Cultivating Your Identity from Seed to Harvest

Freedom in the Light
Engaging the Truth That Sets You Free

www.kingslantern.com

CPSIA information can be obtained
at www.ICGtesting.com
Printed in the USA
LVOW13s0432190917
549182LV00012B/128/P